Stained Glass Patchwork Tec[hniques]

Introduction

ONCE upon a time (as all the best books start ...) I tore a page out of a stitching magazine. It was on an almost unknown technique called stained glass patchwork, and as I've always loved both stained glass and interesting fabric art, the strong lines of the design appealed to me. It was only one simple project, but I never forgot its appeal.

Fast forward a good few years, about a decade into my career as an editor and stitcher. I'd been asked to put together a book introducing quilting techniques to beginners: as quilting was still a relatively unknown art to me, I realised that I was perfectly qualified to accept the commission! The American publishers wanted a series of small projects that wouldn't be offputting to new quilters; as always in the publishing world, the deadline for the book was very tight, so I quickly submitted a list of small projects for approval and made up the items. Then, just before I was due to deliver the manuscript, a message came wafting through the air from the other side of the Atlantic: *the publishers have decided that they would like at least one large project. They would like that project to be a bed quilt.*

At this stage, my ignorance stood me in very good stead. By now I was dimly aware that most quilting techniques take a long time – even the fairly simple ones involving machine piecing and/or quilting. I began leafing through books desperately, trying to find a technique which would allow me to create something the size of a bed quilt in the (now absurdly) short time that was still available. And suddenly I remembered the sheet I'd torn out all those years ago.

Amazingly, I managed to find it (not amazing that I still had it; just that I was actually able to lay my hands on it in my hour of need). I studied the instructions for the technique carefully, and decided that it did indeed look both quick and easy. And so it proved to be.

The bright rainbow quilt I made for the book was bold, striking and unique – and *very* quick to put together. My love affair with stained glass patchwork was born. Although I work in many different techniques, stained glass patchwork (or SGP, for short) is the one that I return to again and again.

In 1998 my husband Chris and I published the first UK book on the technique; the books sold like chocolate-pecan brownies fresh out of the oven, and early in 2005, after selling out of its third edition, we

decided that it was time to produce a new guide to the technique. During the intervening years I've developed the method of stained glass patchwork in lots of different ways, and adapted it to create block patchwork, crazy patchwork, foundation-pieced projects and designs created with double-sided bonding web and with machine satin stitch. Fusible bias binding has come onto the market (one of the best inventions in the world; I really should have taken out shares in the company that manufactures it), and wonderful new fabrics are now available that hadn't even been thought of a few years ago.

This book is a chance for me to share some of my discoveries and techniques with you: you'll be astonished at how easy and quick stained glass patchwork is, and how many different effects you can achieve with it. And if you're already familiar with the basic technique, I hope that this book will give you lots of new ideas for ways in which you can vary and adapt it.

Welcome to the world of stained glass patchwork.

The Basic Technique

STAINED GLASS PATCHWORK (SGP) is an exceptionally easy technique, which makes it perfect for beginners, and it's also a very forgiving technique; you can make quite large mistakes and still get away with them! As I mentioned in the introduction, I quickly discovered that SGP is a very quick way of putting together even quite large quilts, because there's no seaming or piecing involved; although it's called stained glass *patchwork*, it's really a method of appliqué. The patches are cut to shape without any seam allowances, then laid on a background (a foundation fabric, the background of your design, or occasionally direct onto a compressed wadding); the edges of the patches are then covered with lines of bias binding. As you stitch on the binding, the raw edges of the fabrics are sealed underneath.

As you look through the pages of this book, you'll see just what an easy – and adaptable – technique it is, and how quickly you get wonderful results. All the way through the the book I'll be teaching you little tips and tricks for getting the most out of the technique. And don't feel that SGP is just a technique for contemporary quilts. Whether you like traditional designs such as the *Fan Cushions* and the *Poppies Picture*, or more contemporary ones such as the *Seascape* or the *Penguin Orchestra*, you'll find that you can get just the kind of result you're looking for in stained glass patchwork.

The same is true whether you like to piece and quilt by hand or machine; you'll find plenty of ideas for both among the projects in this book. And – even better – it's great fun to do!

So, let's begin our exploration of the world of stained glass patchwork at the very beginning: how the basic technique works. All the variations that you'll see throughout the book are just developments of this same basic principle.

Building up the design

1 Start by drawing your design out full-size on plain paper; when you're happy with the design, go over the lines with black felt pen so that they're good and strong. Put numbers on the different parts of the pattern (**a**); this will help you when you're putting all the patches back together again later.

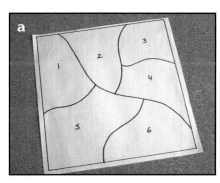

2 Now you need to pick a foundation fabric to build your design on. All of this foundation fabric is going to be covered, so don't bother to use anything smart! Use a light colour – white or cream, ideally – so that you can see the lines of your design through it; sheeting, thin calico (American muslin) and ordinary cotton poplin all work

well. (Occasionally a design can be laid straight onto your background fabric or wadding; if so, the project instructions will mention it.)

3 Cut a piece of background fabric the same size as your design and lay it over the drawing; put a couple of pins in so that the drawing doesn't slip, then trace all the lines of the design in soft pencil (**b**). All of these lines are going to be covered, so you don't need to worry about removing them later. It can be useful to write the numbers in on your foundation fabric too, but if you do this, use a pale crayon, otherwise the numbers may show through any light-coloured fabric patches.

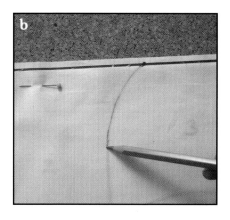

4 Now you need to cut up your original drawing, so if you think you might want to do the same design again, take a photocopy or trace a copy before you cut. Cut along all the marked lines to create templates for cutting the fabric patches (**c**).

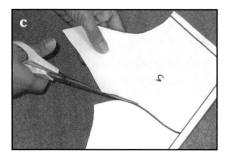

5 The next thing to do is to decide which fabric you're going to be using for which part of the design. If you're not sure straight away, cut a little snippet from each fabric and move them around your design until you're happy with the combination.

6 When you've chosen the fabric for each patch, lay each template right side up on the right side of the fabric and pin it in position, then cut around the edges – or, if you find it easier, you can draw round the template with a pencil and then cut. Remember that, as you're not joining the patches, you don't need to worry about the grain of the fabric and you don't need to add any seam allowances – but if you want to add a little extra safety margin, you can cut just a fraction outside the edges of the template, say 1mm (**d**).

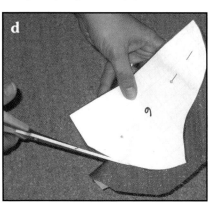

7 When you've cut all the patches out, lay them right side up in their correct positions on the foundation fabric, just like assembling a jigsaw. Once they're all in the right places, pin them in position (**e**). (You can tack/baste them in position if you prefer, but for a design of this size it isn't usually necessary. Besides, I have a pathological aversion to tacking.)

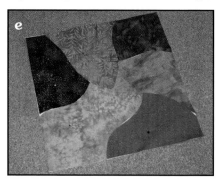

8 You've now assembled your basic design, and it's time to start adding the bias binding! I'll talk about different types of bias binding and tape a bit later, but for now I'm just using standard dressmakers' bias binding, about ⅓in wide – nothing fancy or unusual.

The only thing you need to remember when you're building up an SGP design is to begin with the T-junctions. A T-junction is a line that forms a T-shape with a second line (**f**); as you lay binding

down on the stem of the T, you're going to end up with a raw end of binding where the line stops. If you stitch the binding into position on the stem first, you'll cover the raw end with the crossbar of the T – and so on,

through the design. (If you get it wrong occasionally, it's not a big problem: see the trouble-shooting section on page 78!)

Lay the binding along the line between the two patches, straddling the two fabrics evenly to cover the raw edges, and pulling the binding into nice smooth curves – don't flatten the curves out, but keep them flowing and strong. Pin each section of binding in place; if you pin across the binding, you anchor the fabric each side as well as the binding, and it keeps the work flatter. Also, if you're stitching the binding on by machine, you can stitch over the pins if you're careful, without them keeping on catching in the machine foot. Again, you can tack the binding in place if you prefer, but it's often not necessary for small designs, and tacking just adds work.

9 Once the first lines are pinned in position, you need to stitch down each edge of the bias binding. You can do this by hand or by machine – I'll talk about each method in detail on page 5; for the moment, I'm stitching this design using a small zigzag stitch in a matching thread. Carry on building up the design and covering the raw ends in sequence, working your way through the T-junctions. Once you've stitched all the lines of the design in position (**g**), remove the pins and trim the ends of the bias strips level with the lines they're going into.

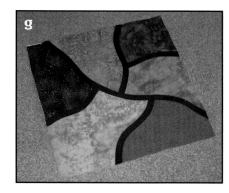

You'll find that on most of the projects in the book I've provided a little sequence of diagrams which shows you the order in which you add the lines of binding. The only exceptions are a couple of the larger projects which feature lots of different lines; by the time you're ready to tackle these designs, you'll be a dab hand at working out the T-junctions for yourself!

Stitching on the binding

I mentioned earlier that you can stitch the binding on by hand or machine. This is mainly just a matter of preference, but it also depends on the finished result you're looking for. I'll show you several different ways, then you can decide which one you like best. So that you can see clearly what's going on, I've stitched some outsize samples using a very wide bias binding; I've also used black thread and very large stitches on a pale binding so that you can see exactly how the stitching looks. Obviously, you'll usually be using a thread that matches your binding – unless you deliberately want a contrast – and your stitching will be rather finer!

Stitching by hand

If you like to stitch by hand, I recommend that you use whatever stitch and stitching technique you would usually use for hand appliqué. I tend to use a slipstitch, working along the bottom of the work, but you may prefer to work along the top line first; do whatever you feel comfortable with. In the finished

outsize sample, there's a line of evenly-spaced slipstitches along each edge of the bias binding (**a**).

Here's a design with the binding stitched on by hand (**b**); it's virtually impossible to see the stitches, not because my stitching's particularly neat, but because it's black slipstitching on a black bias binding.

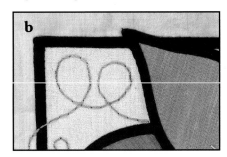

Stitching by machine

Applying the binding by machine is of course much quicker than stitching by hand (although it's not quite so easy to do in front of mindless TV programmes …). By trial and error I've come to the conclusion that, if you prefer stitching by machine, working with a small zigzag works better than using a straight stitch. You'll also find it handy to use an open-toed appliqué foot or a clear appliqué foot if your machine has one; either of these makes it easier to see your stitching line.

Set your machine up for a small zigzag – about 1.5 width and 1.5 length. Try a little sample out to see if you're happy with the look of the stitch. Stitch the inside curve first, positioning the zigzag so that most of it is on the binding but the outside edge just overlaps the edge of the binding (**c**). Go back to the same end of the binding and stitch the outside of the curve, so that you have a neat

line of stitching down each side of the binding (**d**). Working down the binding line in the same direction each time stops the binding from pulling and distorting.

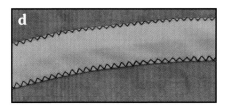

This design (**e**) has been stitched by machine zigzag, although from a distance you can barely see the stitching because again it's black on black.

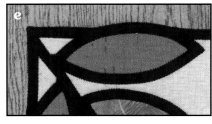

Blind hemming?

Some stitchers like to use the blind hemming stitch on their machine to attach the binding – that's the stitch that makes several straight stitches followed by a V-shape to one side. For this technique, set your machine to the correct stitch; you don't need to use the blind hemming foot – an ordinary zigzag or appliqué foot (or an open-toed/clear one) is fine.

Work the stitching so that the straight stitches are just outside the fold of the binding, and the V-shapes are worked into the fold. With this stitch it isn't usually possible to work the second edge from the same end as the first, as the stitch is asymmetrical, so you'll need to turn the work round and stitch back along the second edge (**f**). (If you're fortunate, you might

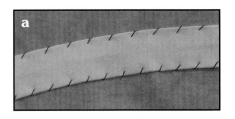

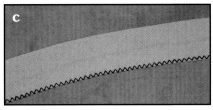

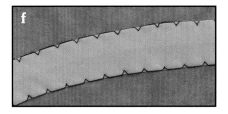

have a machine that flips the stitch from left to right, in which case you *can* work the stitching from the same end again.)

Although this stitch can look more discreet than zigzag, it does mean that quite a large proportion of the stitch is on the fabric patch rather than on the binding; this may be a problem if you're using lots of pale fabrics with dark binding, as the dark thread will show on the fabric patches. If you like the look of the blind hemming stitch, you can overcome this problem by using one of the high-quality invisible machine threads.

Neatening ends

Just occasionally when you're finishing off a stained glass patchwork design you'll have a raw end of bias binding that you can't lose under a T-junction, so you'll need to know how to neaten it. If the line of the design simply comes to an end, fold the raw edge under neatly, either square or at a slight angle, tuck under any little edges that threaten to creep out, then stitch in place as usual (**g** and **h**).

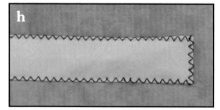

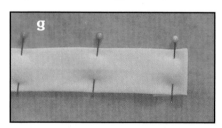

If you have to join two raw ends, for instance to complete a circle, it's best not to overlap them as then you end up with one bumpy side and one flat. Instead, fold both edges under as before and butt them up so that they meet exactly

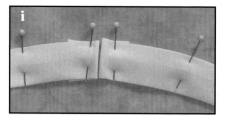

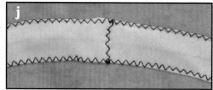

(**i**); stitch down the join, then stitch the outside edges of the binding using your chosen method (**j**).

Making tight curves

Of course the reason for using bias binding for SGP is so that we can use it to cover curved lines; the bias cut allows the strip of binding to take a nice smooth curve. If the curve is quite tight, or if your bias binding is quite firm, hold it in a curve and press it with a steam iron; the steam loosens the fibres and allows them to bend more, and as the binding cools you'll find that it's actually set in its new shape. A quick spray of spray starch before you press also helps this process. In this way you can ease the binding round even quite strong curves (**k**).

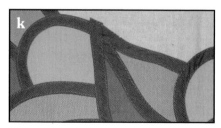

If you need a really tight curve (**l**), just pressing might not be enough. A good solution here is

to gather the inside edge of the binding slightly so that it creates a tight but even curve. Set your machine to the longest straight stitch that it can do, and work a line of stitching along one edge of the binding, just inside the fold. Pull the top thread up gently to create a gather, and even the gathers out with your fingers. Once the curve is tight enough, pin the binding in place on the fabric and attach in the usual way, by hand or by machine (**m**). This helps to keep the curve smooth.

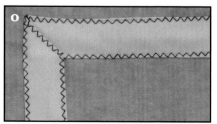

Corners and points

Corners and points are very easy; you just need to make sure that you keep them sharp and well-defined. When you come to a sharp right-angle, you can either fold the binding so that it creates a straight fold (**n**), or mitre it, which is slightly trickier but looks neater (**o**). What you *don't* want is something that's neither one thing nor the other. Make your fold, check that it's nice and sharp and straight, then carry on round the design.

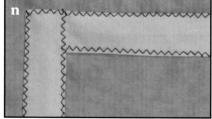

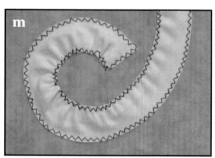

If you're completing a frame shape, cut the binding slightly longer when you come to the final corner (**p**), then fold it under, pin it, and stitch it to conceal the raw edge at the beginning of the binding line (**q**).

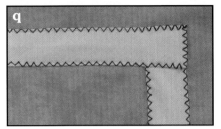

Points are created in the same way as corners, either with a straight fold (**r**), or a mitred fold going down the middle of the point (**s**).

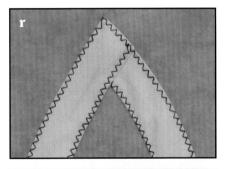

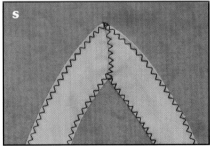

Making tapered points

One extra little technique which you might find useful as you develop your own stained glass designs is making tapered points at the end of lines of binding. Pin the line of bias binding on as usual, then twist the raw end under, pulling it slightly so that you get a smooth curve at the top of the binding line. Pin this twisted

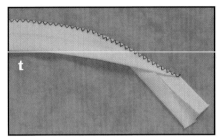

section in place. Stitch down the outside edge of the binding as usual until you reach the point (**t**). When you're ready to stitch back along the other edge, cut the excess binding away with very sharp scissors (**u**); don't cut it away

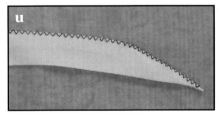

earlier, as the point will fray. Immediately stitch down the point, working a couple of extra stitches if necessary to secure it, then attach the rest of the binding strip (**v**).

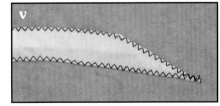

Bindings

Now let's talk about bindings! Bias binding is a strip of fabric which is cut across a fabric's bias grain – that is, at 45° to the straight edges. The bias grain gives the strip of binding flexibility, so that it can be eased around the curves of a design. When you cut a strip of bias fabric – or when it's done by machine – there will be a raw edge on each side of the strip; these edges are neatened by being folded to the wrong side before you use them in stained glass patchwork projects. (If you make your own binding – see below – you might prefer to neaten the edges by making it in tubes rather than folded strips.)

When I'm demonstrating SGP, the question I'm asked most often is whether I make my own bias binding. The answer is that I very rarely bother, for lots of reasons. I've come across many people who've been put off stained glass patchwork for life by going to a workshop where they've spent the first half-day cutting bias strips of black fabric and folding the edges under; by the time lunchtime arrives they've lost the will to live, let alone do anything creative.

My theory is that there are machines whose sole purpose in life is to cut even strips of fabric and fold the edges under, so why should I be responsible for making them redundant and turning them to drink? I couldn't live with that on my conscience … Seriously, though, I don't make my own binding because I'm eager to get on with putting the designs together. If you enjoy making bias binding, though, please do by all means; I know that many people find it soothing to sit in a sunny conservatory listening to a CD and creating lovely yards of binding (actually, when you put it that way, it's beginning to sound quite tempting …)

If you don't want to make your own binding, you'll find that the ones available in the shops are generally good-quality, colour-fast, washable, shrinkproof and available in a wide range of colours, textures and widths. The photographs show just some of these, including cotton and polyester/cotton bindings (**a**), satins (**b**) and metallics (**c**).

The only ones to avoid are the very cheap, loosely-woven bindings that are occasionally on offer on market stalls. These are poor-quality, although at first sight they look quite good because they're stiffened with lots of starch; they are quite translucent, will go very floppy as soon as the starch washes out, and often are not colour-fast.

If you want to use a dark binding for a project and it doesn't have a label saying that it's colour-fast,

it's always worth doing a quick test. Cut a few inches of binding and wet it thoroughly in warm water, then lay it between two scraps of white fabric and press it dry with a hot iron. Check to see if any of the colour has transferred to the white fabric; if it has, either wash the binding first to get rid of all the colour (a drag, but cheaper – and it will spoil the nice sharp folded edges), or use something else (a more expensive option, but much less aggravating …)

Colour

The traditional colour to use for the binding in stained glass patchwork is black, but you can use any colour you like; the important thing is to pick a colour that is a good contrast to your patches, so that you're emphasising the lines of the design. Look at how totally different the same block appears depending on how I've varied the colours in the patches and the binding (**a**).

The iris design (**b** and **c** below) also shows how different the same design can look depending on the fabrics you use and the colour of binding you edge them with; the black binding frames each patch in a dramatic way, while the gold produces a subtler effect.

b

c

d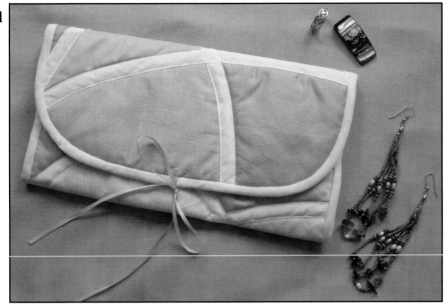

You'll find that I've used various binding colours in the projects in this book, and of course you can use different colours from the ones I've picked.

Pale bias bindings look lovely teamed with pastel fabrics for projects like the little jewellery roll above (**d**). They can look very dramatic against dark fabrics too, but the one thing you have to watch out for is show-through. If you lay white bias binding down on a dark fabric, you'll often find that the fabric shows through the binding; the effect is even worse if you use a wide binding with a large gap between the folds. There are various simple ways to overcome this problem. If your project is small – so you're not spending out too much on the binding – you could try using a double layer; this lessens the show-through dramatically. Or, you can stitch the binding on as usual and then work a line of fancy machine stitching or hand embroidery down the centre of each section (**e**).

e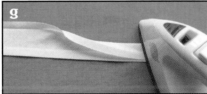

If your binding is quite wide, you could try folding it to a narrower width. Unfold one edge of the binding (**f**), then press it back across the other fold (**g**); the extra layer of fabric will make the binding much more opaque.

f

g

Width

The width of binding I use for many projects is ⅓-½in wide (10-12mm); it's useful for simple designs and medium-to-large items where the patches aren't too small. In this book I've used binding this size on various projects including the *Lavender Sachets* (see page 12), the *Bonbon Cushions* (see page 14), *Beach Huts* (see page 18), *Rainbow Cot Quilt* (see page 31) and *Church Window* (see page 51). When I want binding this width I use ordinary dressmakers'

bias binding (you know, the sort they made you use at school for putting up skirt hems ...); look in dress-fabric shops rather than specialist quilting shops.

If your design is smaller or more detailed, you'll often find that it looks more attractive with a narrower binding so that the patches aren't overwhelmed. In this case ¼in (6mm) binding works well. Binding this width is available in various styles, including a fusible version (see page 38); it's also possible to use ½in binding folded in half if the fabric it's made from isn't too thick. Many quilt supply shops sell narrow bindings in various styles and colours.

Alternatives

Bias binding, with its flexible bias grain, is ideal for stained glass projects, but there are other things that you can use. Some seam bindings are loosely woven and have enough 'give' in them to lie flat around the curves; they're often cheaper than bias binding, too. Upholsterers' braids (**a**) often

a

have a good deal of give in them, too, as they need to be curved round different shapes on furniture, lampshades etc. If you're not sure whether the binding you want to use has enough flexibility, lay a piece of it around the tightest curve of your full-size design – if it lies flat, it will be fine. Wide ricrac also works well.

If your design consists only of straight lines, of course you don't need a binding with any flexibility at all. For this kind of design your choices are much greater; you can try ribbons, strips of fabric, lace, braid, broderie anglaise etc (**b**). For more ideas along these lines, see pages 57-61.

Fabrics

The traditional rule for quilting is that you work in 100% cotton only. Well, who cares about rules? (Never been my strong point …) Cotton fabrics work wonderfully for stained glass patchwork – but so do loads of other fabrics, too. If you're making a project which is going to be laundered often (for instance the *Rainbow Cot Quilt* on page 31), then of course it's a good idea to work with cotton fabrics, but if you're making a decorative wall-hanging or glitzy cushion-cover, anything goes.

And, because you're not seaming or piecing the fabrics, you don't even have to stick to the same fabric within each project: I've done SGP with patches cut from silk, satin, polyester, net, imitation suede, brocade, furnishing fabric, damask, lace and a wide assortment of metallic fabrics – among other things! And, because you don't need to worry about grain, you can often use up scraps of fabric that aren't big enough for conventional patchwork.

You know all those bits of fabric you've bought (or been tempted by) at quilt shows, but can't think how to use? Well, stained glass patchwork could well be your answer. Try pushing your boundaries a little – you could be astonished and delighted by the results you achieve.

Tips for stitching the projects

Now that I've talked you through the basic technique, it's time for you to put theory into practice. The rest of the book is divided into sections; each section covers a different aspect of stained glass patchwork and includes two or more projects using that particular technique. I've given all the projects an easiness rating, to help you decide whether they suit your particular level of skill and experience; if you're a beginner quilter, or new to stained glass patchwork, I suggest that you try a couple of the more straightforward projects before you move on to the more challenging ones.

Sizing things up …

As many of the project templates as possible are full-size, or just require one enlargement on a photocopier. Obviously it isn't possible to put the designs for large wall-hangings etc in at full size; if you have to enlarge a pattern, there are a couple of ways of going about it.

• If you have access to an overhead projector, photocopy or trace the design onto acetate and lay it on the OHP; project it onto a blank wall, adjusting the OHP until the projected image is the size you want it. Tape dressmakers' tracing paper (or, if appropriate, use your foundation fabric) onto the wall, and trace the image in soft pencil.

• Use the grid method. Each of the large designs has a grey grid printed across it (**a**); you might find it useful to add numbers and letters to

identify the rows and columns. On a large sheet of paper, draw out the grid in pencil making each box the size specified on the pattern (**b**), and write in the numbers and letters.

Follow the design to draw in the lines of the design that appear on each part of the grid (**c**); when you've finished, you'll have a full-size version of the design (**d**).

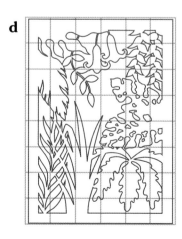

e

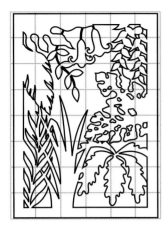

Go over the lines of the design with felt pen to make them stronger and to distinguish them from the gridlines (**e**).

Measuring things up ...

Throughout the projects I've given all measurements in both imperial and metric, so that you can work in whichever system you prefer. Do just choose one and stick with it, though; the measurements aren't always exact conversions, as I've sometimes rounded them up or down to make them more sensible.

Auditioning

No, not for a starring role in the next quilting video: this is a term which describes trying out your fabric choices to see which combination works best. Alongside each project I've included samples of the fabrics that I've used to create it, but you may well want to stitch your designs in totally different colourways. If you're confident with colour, go with your instincts when you're picking fabrics for a particular project.

If you're not, and/or if you have trouble visualising how different fabrics will work in different parts of a particular design, try auditioning them. To do this, cut little snippets of each of your fabrics, then move them around the design in varying arrangements of colour and tone; you'll soon see that some combinations work better than others. If there are too many fabrics of the

same colour or tone in one part of the design, move the snippets around until it looks better. If one particular fabric really doesn't seem to go, swap it for something else – or find an extra fabric with a print that includes all the colours you want to use, and so makes a visual 'bridge' between them.

If you feel like trying a totally new colourscheme, there are various ways in which you can get inspiration.

- pick a strongly-patterned or painted fabric that includes a wide range of colours, then choose other fabrics to tone with it (**a** and **b** show two totally different results of this method).

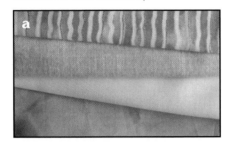

- if you have a collection of anything (buttons, embroidery threads, paperclips, aardvarks ...) in lots of different colours, put them together and pull a few out at random. They might produce some striking colourschemes that you wouldn't have thought of (**c**).

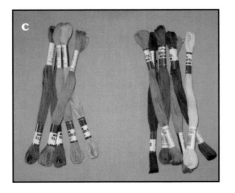

(If the colours are ones that look totally ghastly together, pretend you didn't see them and put them back for another go.)

- have a look around; you'll find some of the most lovely and unusual colourschemes in nature.

When in doubt, read the instructions ...

Whatever your level of experience, I do suggest that if you want to stitch a particular project, you read all the way through the requirements and the instructions before you start. You'll find that I've included all kinds of helpful tips and pointers along the way; also, some projects are assembled or finished in different ways from others, or stages are worked in a different order. If you familiarise yourself with the whole process before you start, you'll be more confident as you stitch.

Having said that, though, the projects are only intended as springboards for your own creativity; I want you to make them yours, adding your own personal touches and skills to the basic designs. And don't forget, if you make a stained glass project that you're particularly pleased with, I'd love to see a photograph of it; you'll find my contact details on page 104.

So, now it's over to you!

Starter Projects

AS you'd expect from the title, this section contains a couple of very straightforward projects. There are no T-junctions (see page 4), and the designs are created using simple patches and just a few lines of bias binding. If you're a total beginner (to quilting or to stained glass patchwork), these projects will show you just how easy the technique is; try them first, and they'll give you the confidence to experiment with some of the other ideas in the book.

Lavender Sachets

Finished size:
each sachet is roughly 7in (18cm) square

Easiness rating:
very easy

I used the same selection of batiks and prints for all my lavender sachets, but varied their positions on the design

THIS is a perfect project for trying out stained glass patchwork; even if you're a beginner, the design is so easy that you could make several of these little lavender sachets in a weekend. As there are no T-junctions in this design, it doesn't matter in which order you add the lines of bias binding.

I've suggested two main ways in which you can finish off the sachets, either by making them up like softly-stuffed pincushions, or by binding the edges with wider bias binding. And, if you feel adventurous, you can add hand embroidery or even some beads or buttons for extra embellishment once the sachet is made up.

You will need:

for each sachet

➤ 7in (18cm) square of foundation fabric

➤ 7in (18cm) square of backing fabric

➤ nine different plain or print fabrics in shades of blue/lavender/turquoise, 4in (10cm) square of each

➤ 1yd (1m) bias binding in a contrasting colour, ½in (12mm) wide when folded

➤ If you're binding the sachet: 1yd (1m) matching bias binding, 1in (2.5cm) wide when folded

➤ sewing thread to match the binding

➤ small amount of dried lavender

➤ soft pencil and pale crayon

➤ polyester stuffing (or two 7in /18cm squares of compressed wadding, if you're binding the sachet)

➤ hand embroidery threads and/or beads for embellishing (optional)

Instructions

Making the stuffed sachet:

1 Trace or photocopy the template on page 79. Lay the square of foundation fabric over the design and trace the lines in pencil; draw in the numbers in pale crayon (**a**).

2 Decide which fabric you'd like to use for which section of the design. Cut up the paper design and use each piece as a template to cut a patch from the appropriate fabric; remember to use the templates right side up on the right side of the fabric. Pin the patches in position on the foundation fabric (**b**).

3 Add the lines of narrow bias binding one at a time (**c**), stitching either by hand or machine.

4 Put the SGP design and the square of backing fabric right sides together; stitch a ½in (12mm) seam all the way around the square, leaving roughly 4in (10cm) open for turning (**d**). Clip the corners and turn the design right side out; fill softly with the stuffing, slipping the dried lavender into the centre of the stuffing. Close the turning with ladder stitch or slipstitch to complete the sachet, and embellish with a few beads or hand embroidery if you wish (**e**).

a

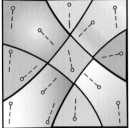

b

c

d

e

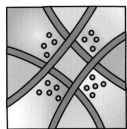

Making the bound sachet:

1 Follow steps 1-3 above to create the front panel of the sachet. Lay the square of backing fabric right side down on a flat surface and cover with one square of wadding. Put the lavender in the centre of the wadding square, then cover with the second square of wadding and finally the SGP design, right side up. Tack the layers together about 1in inside the raw edges, then round off the corners evenly (**f**).

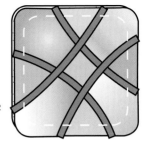

f

2 Unfold one edge of the wider bias binding and lay it right side down around the edge of the design, aligning the raw edges; fold the raw ends of the binding over for about ½in (12mm) where they butt up (**g**). Stitch by machine along the fold line, then fold the binding to the back and slipstitch it in place; close the gap where the ends of the binding join with ladder stitch to complete the sachet (**h**).

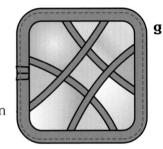

f

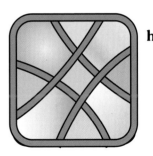

g

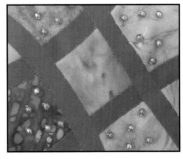

h

I've used small beads to embellish some of the sachets

TIP

I bought a 'sampler' pack of batiks from a quilt shop to give me the main fabrics for these sachets.

Bonbon Cushions

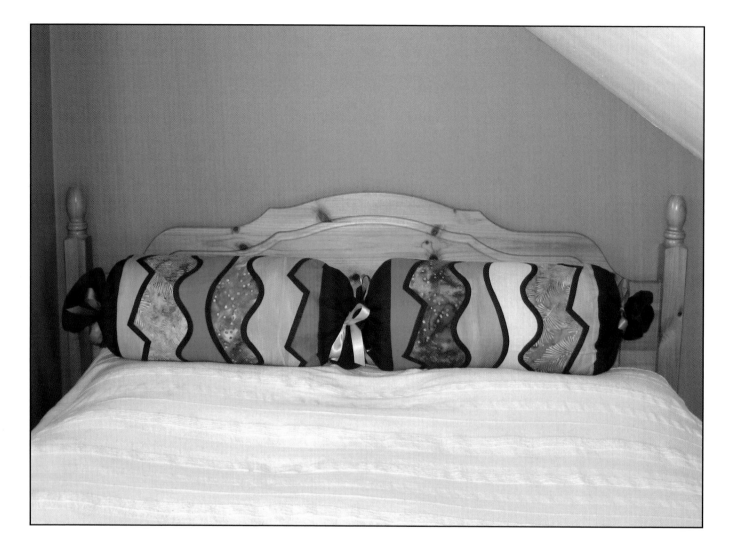

Finished size:
each cushion is roughly 22in (56cm) long (including tied ends) and 28in (70cm) in circumference

Easiness rating:
easy

*T*HESE bright and bold cushion-covers, tied over bolster-shaped stuffings, look like multicoloured bonbons – an effect that's enhanced by the ribbon ties at the ends. Once again there are no T-junctions in this design, so it's very straightforward; this project also gives you the chance to try out some corners as you stitch the bias binding over the zigzags. Use a mixture of bright fabrics in plains and prints; if you make two or more cushion covers in the same design, as I've done here, you could use a slightly different combination of fabrics on each.

You will need:

for each cushion

➤ black cotton background fabric 38 x 30in (97 x 75cm)

➤ six brightly-coloured fabrics, 30 x 6in (75 x 15cm) strip of each

➤ two 28in (70cm) lengths of wide ribbon in bright colours

➤ bolster cushion pad, 18in (45cm) long and 28in (70cm) in circumference

➤ 7yd (7m) black bias binding, ½in (12mm) wide when folded

➤ large sheet of paper 30 x 18 (75 x 45cm)

➤ pencil, long ruler, felt pen

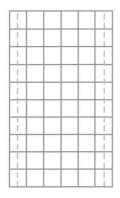

a

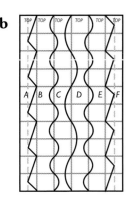

b

I used these fabrics in different combinations for the two cushion covers

Instructions

1 Using the pencil and long ruler, divide the paper rectangle into 3in (7.5cm) squares; you'll end up with a grid of six squares by ten squares (**a**). Using the design on page 82 as a guide, draw in the curved and zigzag lines. The exact sizes of the curves and zigzags aren't important, as long as they're fairly even along each line. Go over the lines of the design with felt pen, and mark the top of each section as shown on the template (**b**).

2 Cut along the felt pen lines to create six individual templates. Decide which of your fabrics you'd like to use for which part of the design, then use the paper templates to cut shapes from the appropriate fabrics (**c**); remember to use the templates right side up on the right sides of the fabrics.

3 Fold the black fabric in half across its width and press the fold; unfold. Lay it right side up on a flat surface and, beginning 9in (23cm) to the left of the centre fold, pin the fabric shapes in position (**d**).

4 Pin and stitch bias binding over the joins between the patches and over the straight edges of patches A and F (**e**). Keep the curves smooth and even, and the straight lines and corners nice and crisp.

5 Fold under and stitch a small double hem at the sides (shorter edges) of the black fabric panel. Fold the design into a long tube, right sides together, and stitch a ½in (12mm) seam along the long edges (**f**); don't worry about trying to make the edges of the patches join perfectly. Press the seam open and turn the tube right side out.

6 Slip the bolster inside the tube and position it centrally; use the lengths of ribbon to gather each end of the tube against the end of the bolster, and tie in a floppy bow (**g**).

> ### TIP
> Use sheets of newspaper for making up your pattern; stick several sheets together with sticky tape if necessary.

c

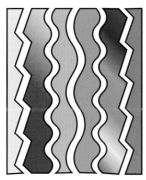

d

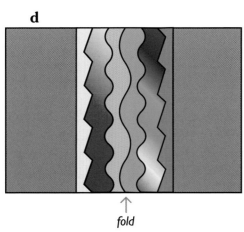

↑
fold

e

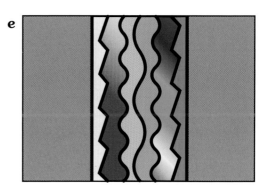

f

g

Quilting by Hand and Machine

As quilters, we're not satisfied just with flat piecing and appliqué: we want to live up to our name. We want to quilt our work too! One of the many things I like about stained glass patchwork is that, if you want, you can quilt the work as you go. Of course, if you prefer, you can quilt it afterwards, by hand or machine – we'll explore that idea in the projects in this section. First of all, though, I'll show you how you can combine the SGP and the quilting in one process; a version of the technique known as quilt-as-you-go.

These days there are almost as many kinds of wadding (batting) around as there are fabrics! Don't let them confuse you; if you're not sure what kind of wadding to use, pick one that you've tried and liked before, or use a basic 2oz polyester wadding that is a good all-purpose wadding.

If you use quite a squashy (high-loft) wadding, it's best to use a backing of muslin or some other fabric to make a complete three-layer sandwich; the three layers pulling together as you stitch them creates a good quilted look. If you use one of the flatter, more felted waddings such as a firm cotton or one of the more compressed polyester waddings, you won't necessarily need a muslin backing – try it with and without, and see what you prefer. I'm a great believer that the best quilting technique for you is often simply what you feel most comfortable doing.

Quilt-as-you-go

1 Begin by tracing the basic design on a foundation fabric, just as for the basic SGP process (see page 3).

2 If you're using a backing, lay this down on a flat surface and cover it with the wadding, then lay the design right side up on top of the wadding. Cut your fabric patches and pin them in place through all the layers (**a**).

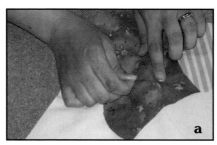

3 If you prefer, you can stitch while the layers are pinned together, but if it's a large piece of work it's often easier to tack the layers together (**b**), to

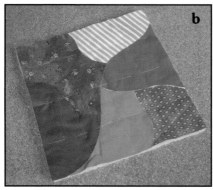

hold them in position while you're quilting – if you don't like tacking you can use safety pins, or a tack gun that shoots little plastic tags through the layers, or a very light spray of one of the glues sold specially for quilt use.

4 Adding the bias binding is done in exactly the same way as for the basic technique – beginning with the T-junctions (**c**) and working your way through the design. The only difference is that now, as you stitch on the binding, you're quilting as you stitch. As ever you can stitch by hand or by machine; if you stitch by hand, take your slipstitches through all the layers to give a good quilted effect.

Here's how the block looks now I've stitched on all the lines of binding (**d**). I've used the technique of quilt-as-you-go for projects such as the *Penguin Orchestra* (see page 43), *Christmas Star Table-Mat* (see page 36), and *Four Seasons Wall-Hanging* (see page 40).

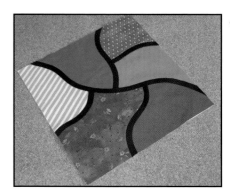

Working straight on the wadding

If your design is very simple, you may be able to lay it directly on the wadding (**e**) instead of using a foundation fabric. This works particularly well if you're using one of the modern compressed waddings; the patches don't bounce around on the top the way they do with the more springy, high-loft waddings. In this case, skip the stage of tracing the design, and simply use the wadding where I've mentioned the foundation fabric in the sequence above.

Quilting after the binding

You may prefer to quilt your project by hand or machine, or to add more texture, *after* you've added the binding. If you want to quilt in this way, the world is your oyster; you can use virtually any hand or machine quilting technique on stained glass patchwork projects, but here I'll show you just a couple of ideas to get you started.

Quilting by hand

Traditional hand quilting works just as well on stained glass patchwork as it does on any other patchwork technique; on the *Church Window* design (see page 51) I've worked traditional hand quilting around the *edge* of each patch of exotic fabric (**a**).

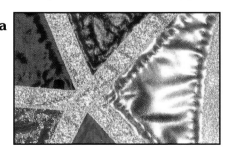

Big-stitch quilting in coton perlé is one of my favourite quilting techniques, because it grows very quickly and gives a slightly embroidered effect to the surface; I've used big-stitch quilting to emphasise the strong line of the silhouette on *It's a Jungle out There …* (see page 70). On the foundation-pieced *Seascape* (see page 75) I chose traditional hand-quilting for the texture lines in the sky, and big-stitch quilting for the stronger lines of the sea.

In recent years quilters have discovered the concept of hand-quilting with embroidery stitches; Nikki Tinkler has been particularly influential in this area, with her Quilting With A Difference technique. I've used this idea on the hand-quilted cushion-cover (see page 34), where I've used random cross-stitches and wavy lines of wheatear stitch (**b**).

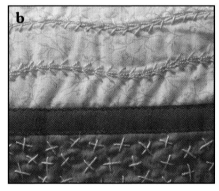

You can also quilt by stitching beads, buttons, sequins etc through all three layers, as I've done on the *Herb Cushion* (see page 60); on the *Crazy Cushions* (see page 58), I've combined hand-embroidery and beading.

Quilting by machine

If you don't fancy the idea of quilting by hand, there are all kinds of ways in which you can add texture to your projects by machine. One very simple way is to stitch lines of straight or fancy stitching along different areas of your design. You can use a special walking foot for machine quilting, but for small projects and simple lines like this you don't really need one.

Vermicelli or stipple stitching (**c**) is a popular way of adding texture by machine. Some quilters are a bit afraid of free machining, but it's really very easy; try out a few practice pieces to get into a smooth flow. For any type of free machine quilting, you want the fabric to be able to move freely under the machine foot, so you need to drop the feed dogs (that's the wonderful name for those little teeth that feed the fabric under your machine foot straightly and evenly), and also to use the darning foot. The trick is to make the stitching look random, while actually covering the fabric fairly evenly.

And of course there are many other ways in which you can add texture by machine; on the *Iris Landscape* (see page 54) I've added lines of texture to the sky and watery lines to the river; on *Fish Supper* (see page 25) I've used various types of machine quilting, including overlapping loops, triangular spirals, and a combination of vermicelli, fish-shapes and the names of different types of seafood! Try out different patterns of free machining, lines of straight and fancy stitches, following the lines of your patches or stitching straight across them – some things will work, others won't, but you'll never know till you try …

Beach Huts

Finished size:
21 x 15in
(53.5 x 38cm)
Easiness rating:
easy

*E*VOKE *the seaside delights of a gentler age in this whimsical wall-hanging. Stitch your own line of candy-striped beach huts hugging the shoreline; choose nice brightly-striped fabrics in a range of colours. If you're quite new to stained glass patchwork, this simple design will teach you how to work with straight lines, curves, corners and points.*

The stitching can be done by hand or machine, although of course machine will be quicker. Once the wall-hanging is complete you can add extra quilting by hand or machine if you wish, plus cheerful buttons for the door handles; embellishments such as shells, beads, pebbles or scraps of net add the final seasidey touch.

Pick bright striped fabrics for the beach huts to contrast well with the sky, sand and sea and to give the panel a 1930s feel

You will need:

➤ cotton fabrics as follows:
- 'sky' fabric 21 x 10in (55 x 26cm)
- 'sand' fabric 21 x 5in (55 x 13cm)
- pale aqua 'sea' fabric 15 x 5in (38 x 13cm)
- mid aqua 'sea' fabric 21 x 7in (55 x 18cm)
- four different brightly-striped fabrics for the beach huts, one 9in (22cm) square of each
- four different bright plain cottons for the doors, one 5in (12cm) square of each
- plain backing fabric in a colour to match your bias binding, 24 x 18in (61 x 46cm)

➤ compressed polyester wadding 21 x 15in (55 x 38cm)

➤ 4yd (4m) bias binding, ½in (12mm) wide when folded. (I've used brown, which goes nicely with the other colours of the beach scene, but you can use black or any other contrasting colour if you prefer)

➤ 2½yd (2.5m) white bias binding, ½in (12mm) wide when folded (if your white bias binding is very translucent, buy twice the amount so that you can use it double)

➤ sewing threads to match the bias binding colours

➤ four round buttons in bright colours for the door handles

➤ ½yd (50cm) white lace or broderie anglaise for the sea foam (optional)

➤ aqua and yellow threads for hand or machine quilting (optional)

➤ beads, scraps of net or mesh, shells, pebbles, seasidey beads etc for embellishment (optional)

➤ ruler and soft pencil, clear sticky tape

Instructions

1 Photocopy the two parts of the template on pages 80-81 and tape them together. Lay the wadding on a flat surface and put the piece of 'sky' fabric at the top; pin it in position (**a**).

a

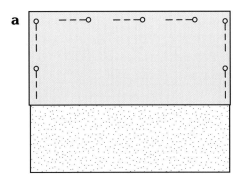

2 Decide which striped fabric you're going to use for each beach hut, and which plain fabric you're going to use for each door. Cut out the templates, and use them to cut patches from the appropriate fabrics for the beach huts, doors, sand and sea sections (remember to use the template shapes right side up on the right side of your fabric each time). Pin these shapes into position on the wadding (the beach huts will overlap the sky fabric), as shown in **b**.

b

3 Add the lines of brown bias binding in the sequence shown, stitching either by hand or machine. Begin with the three straight lines between the huts and the lines around the doors (**c**), then add one long line up the left-hand side, over the roofs and down the right-hand side, keeping the points crisp (**d**).

c

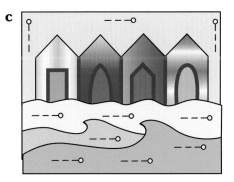

d

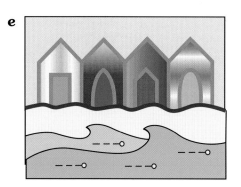

Finish with a wavy line for the top of the sand (**e**).

4 Pin a line of white bias binding along the top of the small wave; if you're using lace or broderie anglaise for the foam, insert this under the crest of the wave as shown (**f**). Stitch the binding in position. Cover the top of the large wave with binding (plus foam) in the same way (**g**).

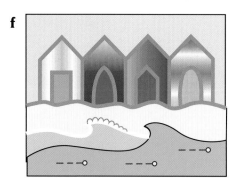

5 Lay the backing fabric right side down on a flat surface and position the design on top of it, right side up, so that there's an even border of brown fabric all the way around. Fold the raw edges over the front of the design in a small double hem and stitch in place by hand or machine (**h**).

6 Stitch the buttons in position on the doors. Add extra hand or machine quilting to the sand and the sea if you wish, and attach any shells or other embellishments in appropriate positions. Add a small casing to the back, loops along the top edge or a couple of curtain hooks for hanging the panel.

TIP

If you don't feel like tackling free machine-quilting, leave the panel just as it is, or add a few lines of hand-quilting in toning colours across the sand and the sea.

Swirling spirals of machine quilting suggest water; the sand is quilted with loose curved shapes. Shells and scraps of net enhance the seaside feel of the design.

Seashells Sofa Throw

Finished size:
28in (71cm) square

Easiness rating:
fairly easy

*A*NOTHER celebration of the seaside, this time using large shell and sealife shapes embellished with various styles of hand quilting. I've used hand-dyed fabrics for the sand and the seawater border so that they give a random effect across the large patches of fabric, but any of the slightly mottled or marbled cotton prints on the market would work well. This design would also look good with the shells and animals appliquéd in shades of pink/orange/terracotta.

Hand-dyed fabrics produce a pretty random effect on the 'sand' and 'sea' patches.

You will need:

- ➤ cotton fabrics as follows:
  - blue/green 'sea' fabric 28in (70cm) square
  - yellowy 'sand' fabric 23in (59cm) square
  - mottled mauve for the nautilus shell 15in (38cm) square
  - mid aqua for the starfish 13in (33cm) square
  - pale turquoise for the long shell 15 x 8in (38 x 20cm)
  - mottled pale brown for the crab 21 x 14in (53 x 36cm)
- ➤ compressed wadding 28in (70cm) square
- ➤ brown backing fabric 30in (75cm) square
- ➤ 12yd (12m) brown bias binding, ⅓in (8mm) wide when folded
- ➤ brown sewing thread to match the binding
- ➤ quilting threads in colours to tone with the fabrics
- ➤ 28in (70cm) square of plain paper
- ➤ pencil, ruler, felt pen, chalk marker

Instructions

1 Use the grid method (see page 10) to enlarge the template on page 83; go over the lines with felt pen to make them darker. Lay the square of 'sand' fabric right side up over the design so that there's an even border of fabric all round the central

square of the design; pin in place, then trace all the outlines of the design with soft pencil (**a**). Don't bother with the internal lines, as these will just get covered up by the fabric patches.

2 Cut the crab, starfish and shell shapes out of the paper template (the rest of the template can be discarded), then use these to cut shapes from the appropriate fabrics; remember to use the templates right side up on the right sides of your fabrics.

Use the chalk marker to draw in the internal lines on the patches (**b**), either by eye, or by laying the shapes over the paper templates on a lightbox. Pin the fabric shapes in position on the traced design, then go over the raw edges with a small zigzag to secure the patches (**c**).

3 Lay the square of 'sea' fabric right side up on a flat surface and position the design, right side up, on top so that there's an even border of fabric all the way around. Stitch a line of small zigzag all the way around the silhouette of the design – that is, round the pencil square, and round any parts of the design that extend beyond the square (**d**). Carefully cut the excess yellow fabric away from the edges of the design to reveal the border fabric (**e**); on the reverse of the work, carefully cut the excess border fabric away from behind the design.

4 Lay the square of wadding out on a flat surface, then position the design on top, right side up, so that the raw edges align. Follow the sequence shown in **f** to add the lines of bias binding, stitching the binding on either by hand or by machine.

5 Lay the square of backing fabric right side down on a flat surface and position the design on top of it, right side up, so that there's an even border of brown fabric all the way around (**g**).

Secure the layers together using your favourite method – tacking, tack gun, quilt glue, safety pins etc.

6 Now it's time to add different types of hand quilting to give the different parts of the design their own flavour.

First of all, outline each patch of coloured fabric with a line of hand-quilting about a quarter of an inch inside the bias edge; then do the same outside the shapes, on the sandy-coloured background fabric.

Emphasise the shapes of the two shells by stitching partial lines of quilting in each patch to echo the lines of bias binding (**h**).

On the starfish, stitch curvy lines radiating out from the centre and along each arm, and little curved lines in between (**i**).

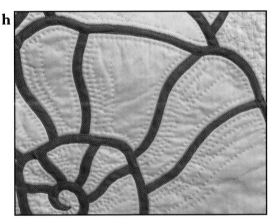

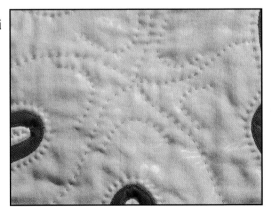

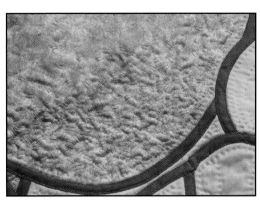

To create a random texture on the crab shell, stitch pairs of little straight seeding stitches at different angles (**j**); work lots of them concentrated at the back of the shell, then make the gaps between the stitches larger towards the front of the shell.

Stitch single lines of straight seeding stitches at different angles on the yellow background fabric, to create an attractive allover texture; finally, to suggest the effect of water on the border fabric, stitch a series of wavy lines of quilting in greens and aquamarines (**k**).

7 Once all the hand quilting is complete, fold the raw edges over the front of the design in a small, even double hem and stitch in place by hand or machine.

TIP

A chalk marker is best for marking the internal lines on the fabric patches, as the lines can easily be rubbed out if you don't get them in exactly the right places! You might also want to use your chalk marker for the quilting lines on the shells and starfish.

Fish Supper

Finished size:
42 x 54in
(102 x 137cm)

Easiness rating:
challenging – there are
lots of different pieces
in this quilt, and lots
of lines of bias binding,
so think of it as a
long-term project

I chose the plain fabrics at
the bottom of this
selection first, then picked
out lots of toning fabrics in
darker shades and
matching prints.

I'VE been wanting to design a quilt
featuring a quirky cat for quite a
while, and when I began working on
this book it seemed the ideal time.
I felt the cat ought to be surrounded
by brightly-coloured fish, so it
seemed a short jump from that idea
to work out just what the cat had
been doing with some of the fish ...
hence the quilt's title! I've gone over
the top with the machine quilting on
this design (see some of the close-up
photographs on page 27), but you
can quilt it much more simply if you
prefer, either by hand or by machine.

You will need:
➤ cotton fabrics as follows:
- cream background fabric 42 x 54in
  (102 x 137cm)
- mauve backing/binding fabric 47 x 61in
  (120 x 155cm)
- fabric for the cat's body and head 32 x 15in
  (80 x 40cm)
- darker fabric for the back and tail 24 x 18in
  (60 x 45cm)
- contrast fabric for the zigzag detail on the
  back and tail 24 x 18in (60 x 45cm)
- four or five plain fabrics for the larger
  border backgrounds, roughly ½yd (50cm)
  of each to provide plenty of choice
- lots of large scraps of plain, print and
  mottled fabrics to tone in with your
  colour-scheme; these will be used for the
  smaller border panels and to create the
  fish and fishbones
➤ compressed wadding 42 x 54in
  (102 x 137cm)
➤ 38yd (35m) black bias binding, ¼in (6mm)
  wide when folded
➤ black sewing thread
➤ hand or machine quilting threads
➤ six little buttons or large beads for fish eyes
➤ plain paper 42 x 54in (102 x 137cm)
➤ pencil, ruler, felt pen, pale crayon,
  chalk marker

Instructions

1 Use the grid method (see page 10)
to enlarge the template on page
84; go over the lines with felt pen to
make them darker. Lay the cream
background fabric right side up over the
design; pin in place, then use a soft pencil
to trace the outlines of the main cat
sections, the border panels and the little
decorative shapes (**a**). Don't bother with

a

the internal lines of the face, or the fish
and fishbone shapes, as these will be
covered up by the fabric patches. Draw in
the letters with a pale crayon (so that they
won't show through any pale patches).

2 Cut all the border panel shapes
out of the paper design; leave
them whole at this stage – that is, don't
cut out the fish and fishbone shapes.
Cut out the little decorative shapes for
the borders, and the three main sections
of the cat (but again, not the triangles on
its tummy). The rest of the paper design
can now be discarded. Use these paper
shapes as templates to cut patches from

the appropriate fabrics; remember to use the templates right side up on the right sides of your fabrics. When you're cutting out the main shape for the cat, don't forget to cut out the eye sections so that the cream background fabric can show through; keep the circles for the pupils and cut them from a contrasting fabric. Pin all the plain border shapes (that is, the ones that don't have fish or fishbones on them), the small decorative patches and the three main cat pieces in position on the cream fabric (**b**), then secure them in place with a small zigzag stitch.

b

3 Mark each large border panel on the back with the pale crayon so that you know which one is which and which way up it goes. Now cut up one of the fish shapes into its individual sections, and use these paper pieces as templates to cut patches from your chosen fabrics; pin these pieces in position on the appropriate background panel (**c**), and secure in place with a small zigzag. Do the same with the other five fish panels. On the fishbone panels, draw in the skeleton then add fabric patches for the heads and tails (**d**).

c

d

4 Remembering the T-junctions (see page 4), build up the lines of binding on each fish. In sequence **e**, I've shown you the order for one of the fish to remind you how it works! For the fishbones, follow the sequence shown in **f**.

e   **f**

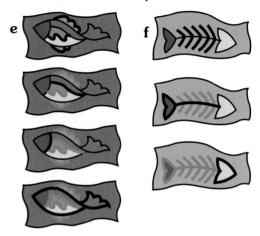

5 Cut the triangles out of the paper cat template and use these to cut patches from a contrasting fabric (or you could use several different fabrics if you prefer): pin these in place on the cat's tummy, and secure with zigzag. Use the chalk marker to draw in the facial details, and cut and position the pupils of the cat's eyes,

g

plus the nose, tongue and the insides of the ears. Then (remembering the T-junctions) add the lines of binding to the cat design (**g**). Don't put in the whiskers at this stage; they'll be added after quilting.

6 Pin the decorated border panels into position on the design and secure each one with a small zigzag. Now add the lines of binding around and between the borders, and around the decorative shapes (**h**). Don't add binding to the outer wiggly line yet.

h

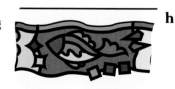

7 Lay the backing fabric out on a flat surface, right side down, and lay the wadding on top so that there's an even border of fabric all the way around. Position the design on top of the wadding, right side up, so that there's an even border of wadding all the way around the design (**i**).

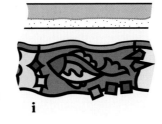

i

Secure the layers together using your favourite method – tacking, tack gun, quilt glue, safety pins etc – then quilt as you wish by hand or machine. Whichever method you're using, begin in the centre of the design and work outwards; leave the final narrow border unquilted at this stage so that you can tuck the binding fabric underneath it at the next stage.

8 Carefully trim the edges of the wadding so that they are straight and the corners are square; be very careful not to cut the backing fabric as you do this. Fold the raw edges of the backing fabric over the front of the design, trim them slightly if necessary, and tuck them under the edges of the narrow border. Tack or pin securely in place, then add a final line of bias binding down the raw edge of the narrow border (**j**). Finish by quilting the narrow border by hand or machine.

j

9 Stitch the whiskers in position. Embellish the quilt with a few buttons or beads if you wish, and add some bead eyes to the fish. Add a casing to the back of the quilt for hanging.

> ## TIP
> Stitching each of the fish panels separately is much easier than trying to add all the fabric patches and bias binding lines to the complete quilt.

As you can see from the details below, I've had a lot of fun machine-quilting this design! I quilted most of the coloured patches within the lines in different patterns, and stitched a mixture of vermicelli quilting, sealife shapes and fish names on the cream background.

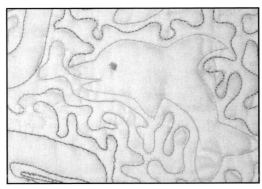

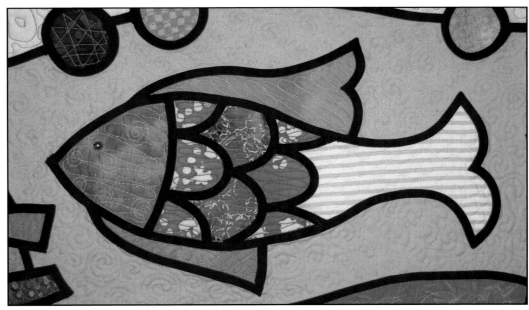

Stained Glass Blocks

ALTHOUGH lots of the designs I stitch are contemporary, I love the look of traditional block patchwork too – but one of the reasons I don't do it very much is because my stitching is rather slapdash! In order to make traditional blocks that look really good, you have to be pretty careful in the way you measure and cut the patches, and then stitch them in accurate quarter-inch seams so that all the points match up – I never seem to have the patience and the accuracy to make them work out properly. So, if you're like me, I'm going to show you a way of creating traditional-looking patchwork with much less hassle and in a fraction of the time.

All you do is simply treat each block the way we do ordinary stained glass patchwork; cutting out patches without seam allowances, and then using binding or tape to cover the joins. No seaming, no piecing, no matching of seams or points – and a load of fun to do!

And, if you stitch the patches onto wadding squares (see page 17), you're quilting as you go – which saves even more hassle and time because you don't have to stretch, tack (baste) and quilt a whole quilt top when you've done the patchwork.

If you're using a design such as Pinwheel or Shoofly, where all the lines are straight, you could use tape, ribbon or even strips of fabric or lace instead of bias binding (see page 57); you only need the stretch of the bias when you have to ease the binding round curved lines such as the quarter-circles on Grandmother's Fan blocks.

Creating blocks in stained glass patchwork

1 To create your own block design for SGP, first of all draw out the basic block full-size (**a**). For each different-shaped or

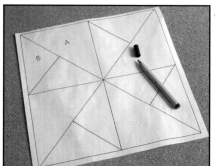

a

different-sized patch in your design, cut out one of the relevant shapes to make a template (**b**), just as you would for ordinary

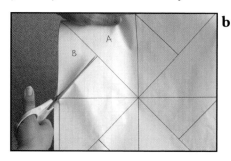

b

patchwork. For this technique, though, you don't need to add any seam allowances, either to the template or to the fabric patches.

2 Use these templates to cut your fabric patches in the usual way for SGP (right sides up on the right sides of your fabrics), as shown in **c**. If you like using a rotary cutter and board, you can cut your patches really quickly just as for traditional patchwork, but remember that you're not adding any seam allowances. Also, unlike traditional patchwork, the grain-

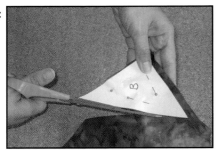

c

line of the fabric isn't important, but do watch out for any straight lines in the designs on printed fabric. If you have straight lines of tape next to slightly crooked printed lines it can spoil the finished look of your piece.

3 When you've cut out all your patches, lay them on your foundation fabric or compressed wadding and pin them in position (**d**). Now you're ready to add the lines of bias binding or tape.

d

4 Just as with ordinary SGP, begin with any T-junctions if your design has them. If the block you're using includes any straight lines, you want the lines of tape to be really straight and crisp. Put a pin in one end of the tape and then stretch it out straight; put a pin in the other end, and you then know that the line is good and level, and you can pin along the middle (**e**).

e

5 Carry on working in in just the same way, building up the design until all the (internal) lines of the block are covered (**f**); don't add any binding around the edges of the block.

f

6 You can even use the same technique for blocks which are part-appliqué, such as Grandmother's Fan. Remember that if your block includes curved lines, as this one does, you'll need bias binding or some other tape that curves rather than straight ribbon. On this design, the lines between the blades of the fan need to be worked first, as they

g

form T-junctions at each end; once these are stitched on (**g**), You can add the curved lines round the top and bottom edges.

Making up a quilt

That's OK, you might be saying, but how do I join the blocks in a quilt once I've done them all? Once again, it couldn't be easier. For the quilt below I made a series of blocks of different kinds. Then I cut a whole series of plain blue squares the same size, laid the blocks out like a chequerboard, and ran long lines of tape down between the rows and then across them to join the blocks into a whole quilt. Voilà: a traditional-looking quilt top in the fraction of the time it would take you to piece it the traditional way!

If you want to use more of the decorative blocks, you might prefer to space them out by joining them with sashing and corner blocks. You can then layer the quilt top with wadding and backing, and quilt as you wish.

Other blocks

You can adapt any traditional block design to SGP in the same way; overleaf are just a few of the many blocks that you could experiment with.

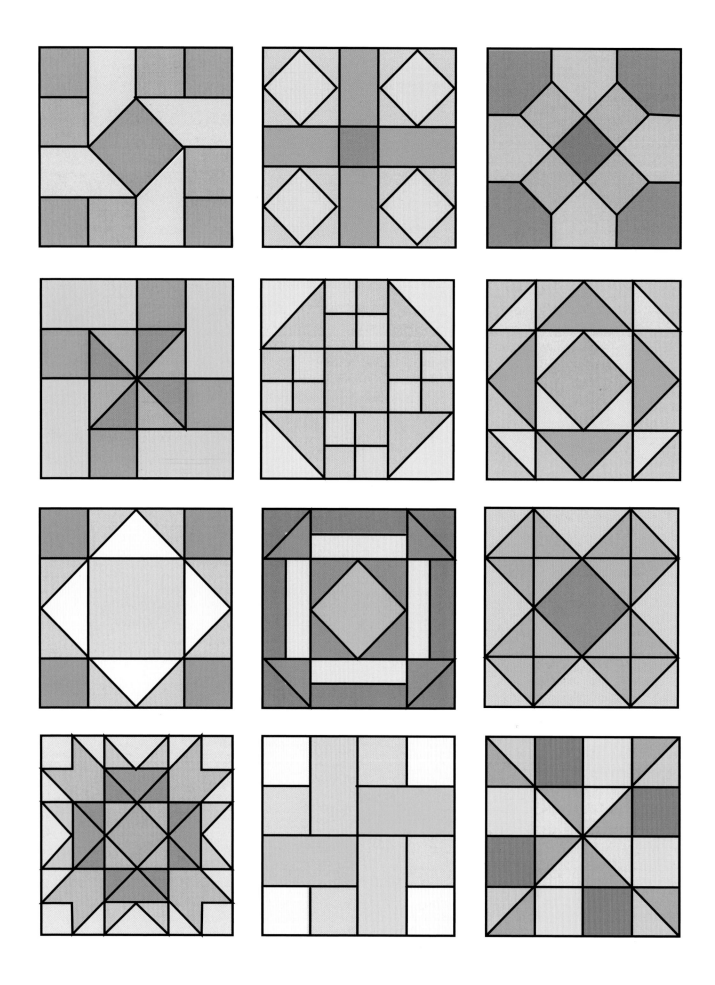

Rainbow Cot Quilt

Finished size:
39 x 51in
(100 x 130cm)

Easiness rating:
medium

The bright fabrics I used for my cot quilt all feature slight patterns

*P*AINT a rainbow in the sky for a special baby's cot. This design uses the simple patchwork block known as Roman Stripes or Amish Stripes; using stained glass patchwork it's even quicker than usual to put together. Because all the lines joining the patches are straight, you can use ribbon, tape or seam binding instead of bias binding if you prefer. I've chosen slightly mottled fabrics for the rainbow patches rather than absolute plains, and I've given them even more visual interest with a small amount of machine quilting. If you'd prefer a subtler colour-scheme, choose pastels or mid-tones instead of brights for the rainbow patches; if you'd like it even brighter than my version (!), pick a multicoloured print instead of the sky/cloud design.

You will need:

- ➤ twelve 12in (30cm) squares of sky fabric
- ➤ twelve different rainbow fabrics, one 12in (30cm) square of each
- ➤ black backing/binding fabric 41 × 53in (100 × 135cm)
- ➤ machine quilting threads to match each of the rainbow fabrics
- ➤ compressed wadding 39 × 51in (100 × 130cm)
- ➤ 35yd (35m) of black tape or seam binding, ½in (12mm) finished width
- ➤ black sewing thread
- ➤ rotary cutter, board and rule

Instructions

1 Stack the squares of rainbow fabrics in sixes, working through the colours of the rainbow in order, then cut them in half diagonally (**a**). Put one half of each square aside, then cut the remaining triangles into 2in (5cm) strips, measuring in from the long edge each time (**b**). The final small triangle will be slightly wider than 2in (5cm).

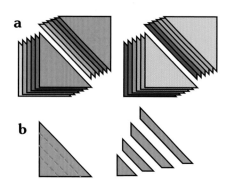

2 Put the strips into piles of twelve, so that each pile works its way through the rainbow (**c**). Following the layout shown (**d**), pin the strips onto the corners of the sky fabric.

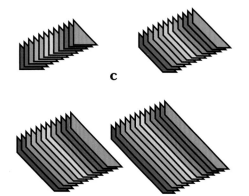

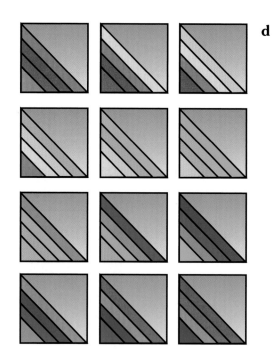

(If your sky fabric has a one-way print, make sure that each square is the correct way up.) Put strips of binding/tape across the joins between the patches, and the final edge of the longest strip, and stitch them in place by hand or machine (**e**).

3 Use a medium zigzag to join the blocks as shown to create the quilt top (**f**); don't add binding to these lines yet.

4 To create the border, cut the remaining bright triangles in half to create wide strips (**g**); sub-cut some of these strips to

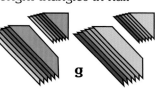

create random lengths (**h**). Join these pieces with binding/tape to create four border strips, mixing up the sizes of the patches so that they don't look too regular. You can either use the colours randomly, or work your way round the rainbow several times, as I've done (this requires a little bit more juggling to ensure that you have a series of complete rainbow sequences).

Once you've joined the patches, cut the strips in half again along their length (**i**);

cutting them into narrower strips at this stage halves the amount of work! Cut the borders to length, then use zigzag to add them round the central block design (**j**); once again, don't add the binding/tape at this stage.

5 Lay the backing fabric, right side down, on a flat surface and position the wadding on top so that there's an even border of fabric all the way around. Position the quilt top on top of the wadding (**k**), and secure the layers together using your favourite method – tacking, tack gun, quilt glue, safety pins etc.

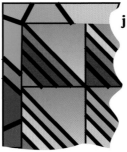

6 Use a simple vermicelli stitch or wave/spiral pattern to quilt along each coloured strip in toning machine quilting thread (**l**). Working the quilting before you add the final pieces of binding/tape means that you can lose the ends of your machine quilting lines underneath the black strips. (Cunning, eh?)

7 Add binding/ tape in a grid design between the patches, and then around the inside edge of the border (**m**). Fold the raw edges of the backing fabric over the front of the design in a small double hem and stitch in place by hand or machine (**n**).

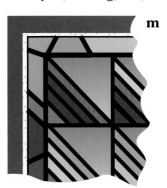

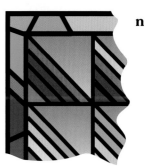

Grandmother's Fan Cushions

Finished size:
each cover is 17in (43cm) square

Easiness rating:
pretty easy

A traditional block is given a modern twist in these two cushion-covers; the fabric square on which the fan design is built becomes part of the design, which eliminates the need for a foundation square. I've used autumnal colours edged with brown bias binding, but of course you could create the design in any colourscheme that matches your own decor.

One of the cushion covers is quilted and embellished by hand in multicoloured silk twist using a variety of stitches; the other version is quilted by machine in various different patterns.

You will need:

for each cushion-cover:

➤ cotton fabrics as follows:
- 12in (30cm) square of background fabric
- four 12 x 3in (30 x 7.5cm) rectangles of sashing fabric
- four 3in (7.5cm) corner squares
- three different fabrics for the fan blades, one 7in (18cm) square of each
- 5in (13cm) square of fabric for the fan centre
- two 18 x 13in (46 x 33cm) rectangles of firm backing fabric

➤ compressed wadding 18in (46cm) square

➤ 4yd (4m) brown bias binding, ½in (12mm) wide when folded, plus toning thread

➤ your own choice of toning hand or machine quilting threads

34

a

Instructions

1 Trace or photocopy the two cushion templates on page 85. Use template A to cut two shapes from each of the fan blade fabrics, and template B to cut a quarter-circle from the fan centre fabric (**a**).

2 Pin the patches in position on the square of background fabric; lay this square in the centre of the wadding square (**b**), and surround it with the sashing squares and rectangles (**c**). Secure all the shapes onto the wadding with a medium zigzag stitch.

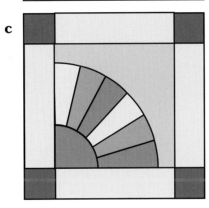

b

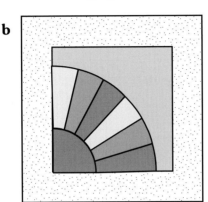

c

3 If you're machine quilting, do this first before you add the bias binding; this way you'll be able to conceal the beginnings and ends of your machining. Once you've completed the quilting as you wish, follow the sequence shown in **d** to add the lines of bias binding.

If you're quilting by hand, you can do this before or after adding the binding – it's up to you.

4 Trim the quilted design to ensure that the edges are even and the corners square. Fold under and stitch a small double hem on one long edge of each backing rectangle (**e**); lay the quilted design right side up, then position the backing pieces on top, right sides down, aligning the raw edges so that the backing pieces overlap (**f**). Stitch a ½in (12mm) seam all the way around, then trim the wadding back to the seam line and clip the corners. Turn the cushion-cover right side out, and press just the very edges to set the seams.

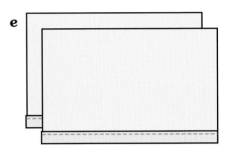

e

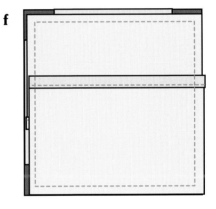

f

> ## TIP
> By making the covers slightly smaller than an 18in (46cm) cushion pad, you'll ensure that the pad stuffs the cushion-cover nice and plumply.

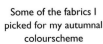

Some of the fabrics I picked for my autumnal colourscheme

d

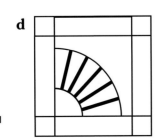
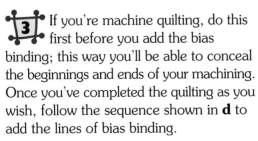
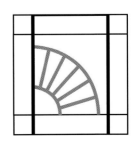
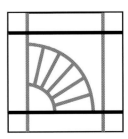

Christmas Star Table-Mat

Finished size:
22in (56cm) square
Easiness rating:
pretty easy

A mixture of prints, plains and metallics looks good in this design

*T*HE lovely star design in the centre of this seasonal table-mat might look complicated, but remember – in stained glass patchwork you don't have to create any sharp points or make any seams match: the binding does all the tricky work for you! I've used a mixture of cotton/metallic prints and plain metallic fabrics; if you choose metallics too, pick the bonded type (the ones that don't fray) rather than lamés. I've edged the shapes with a combination of dark green tape and gold ribbon, but you could use the same colour of binding throughout, or even choose totally different Christmassy colours. How about pale blue, midnight blue and silver? Or purple and gold prints and plains, edged in black?

You will need:

➤ fabrics as follows:
- 16in (40.5cm) square of foundation fabric
- red Christmas print for border 22in (56cm) square
- dark green cotton fabric for backing/binding 24in (61cm) square
- large green/gold print 10 x 6in (25 x 15cm): this is fabric A
- plain red cotton fabric 8in (20cm) square; this is fabric B
- small green/gold print 12 x 6in (30 x 15cm); this is fabric C1
- green/red/gold stripe 2 x 6in (30 x 15cm); this is fabric C2
- metallic red 8 x 4in (20 x 10cm); this is fabric D1
- metallic gold 8 x 4in (20 x 10cm); this is fabric D2
- plain green 8in (20cm) square; this is fabric E

- ➤ compressed wadding 22in (56cm) square
- ➤ 5yd (5m) dark green ribbon or tape, ½in (12mm) wide
- ➤ 2yd (2m) gold ribbon, 1in (2.5cm) wide
- ➤ sewing threads to match the green and gold ribbons

Instructions

1 Trace or photocopy the templates A-E on page 86, and cut out the shapes. Use these templates to cut the following shapes from the various fabrics (remember to place the templates right sides up on the right sides of your fabrics):

- using template A, cut four shapes from fabric A
- using template B, cut four shapes from fabric B
- using template C, cut two shapes from fabric C1 and two from fabric C2
- using template D, cut two shapes from fabric D1 and two from fabric D2
- using template E, cut four shapes from fabric E.

2 Arrange the shapes on the 16in (40.5cm) square of foundation fabric (**a**), following the diagram (**b**) to see how the shapes are positioned. Pin the shapes in place, then secure them with a medium zigzag.

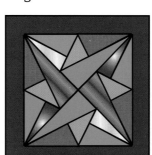

a

b

3 Lay the red border fabric right side up on a flat surface and position the design, right side up, on top so that there is an even border of fabric all the way around (**c**). Stitch a line of zigzag along the edge of the smaller square. On the reverse of the work, carefully cut the excess border fabric away from behind the design.

c

4 Lay the square of wadding on a flat surface and position the design on top, right side up. Secure the layers together using your favourite method – tacking, tack gun, quilt glue, safety pins etc – then follow the sequence shown in **d** to add the lines of green ribbon/tape. Stitch the tape on either by hand or by machine, and keep all the lines nice and straight.

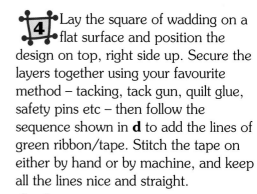

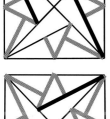
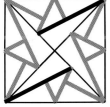
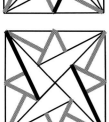

d

5 Add a line of gold ribbon round the edge of the central square (**e**), making sure that the sides are parallel and the corners crisp.

e

6 Lay the green backing fabric right side down on a flat surface and position the design on top of it, right side up, so that there's an even border of fabric all the way around (**f**). Fold the raw edges over the front of the design in a small double hem, making sure that it's even all the way around, and stitch in place (**g**).

f

g

TIP

Building the design up on a foundation square first may seem unnecessary, but it does help to keep the lines of the central design straight and true.

Using Fusible Bias Binding

AS far as I'm concerned, fusible binding is one of the great inventions in quilting, right up there with rotary cutters and foundation piecing! The fusible binding has a little strip of bonding web on the back, protected by a strip of paper; when you're ready to use it, you peel off the paper, lay the binding in position over your line, and fuse it into place with a warm iron, which holds it in position while you stitch. Most of the fusible binding available is ¼in (6mm) wide, which is perfect for small or delicate stained glass patchwork designs; recently a ⅕in (4mm) version has come onto the market, but this is best for other uses such as Celtic designs; it's really too narrow to use for SGP.

Why might you want to use fusible binding, though? And what's the point of making it fusible, if you still have to stitch it in place? For me, this kind of binding gets over several problems in one go. First of all, you've got a ready-made narrow bias binding which is perfect for more detailed SGP designs where you want a slightly finer line – and if you've ever tried making your own binding, you'll know that the narrower it gets, the harder it is to keep it an even width! Because the raw edges are folded under, instead of seamed, it also isn't too bulky. And if you've worked with narrow bias binding before, you'll also know that it's quite hard to pin or tack it in place while keeping good smooth curves.

Being fusible, this binding eliminates any need to pin or tack; as you press it in place it takes a beautiful curve, which it holds perfectly while you stitch it by hand or machine. Also, the bonding web helps to hold the raw edges of the fabric patches in place, which is a bonus if you're using narrow binding. And, it comes in loads of different colours, including a whole range of metallic finishes. The down side is that, in the UK at least, it is pretty expensive; if you live in or visit America, or have any quilting friends who visit you from the US, you'll find fusible binding is much cheaper on that side of the Atlantic. It's extremely easy to use, as you'll see from the sequence below; for these examples I've used the shapes from the *Four Seasons* hanging on page 40.

Applying the binding

1 Follow the steps we went through in the basic technique (see page 4) to draw out your design full-size, cut the fabric patches and assemble them on the foundation fabric (**a**).

a

2 It's particularly helpful when using narrow binding like this to add the scant 1mm on the patches outside the template, and I also find it useful to secure the patches in place with a small zigzag (**b**). The zigzag keeps the

b

patches safely in place so that they can't wriggle while you're adding the binding, and it's both quicker and more secure than tacking (and you don't have to remove the stitches afterwards …)

3 If you wish, add wadding behind the design, and you're ready to begin stitching on the bias binding. As ever, you need to begin with the T-junctions; on this design, that means the lines marked on the first binding diagram. Unpeel the paper from the end of the binding (**c**), and lay

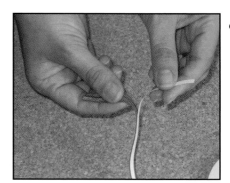

c

d

it at the top of the line; use the tip of a warm iron to fuse it into position (**d**).

Get into the habit of using just the tip of the iron for this process; then, when you're using wadding, you don't flatten it by pressing the whole area. Using just the tip also ensures that you keep the main part of the iron away from delicate fabrics such as sheers and metallics. (If you've got a little mini-iron, you might find it useful for fusing on the binding, but it certainly isn't necessary to buy one specially.)

Ease the binding into place round the lines, stretching it to keep nice strong curves, and pressing each section into place with the iron; trim the binding off at the end of the line. If you make a mistake at any stage, just gently lift the binding off the fabric and reposition it; it's very good-natured, and you can do this several times in a row if necessary.

4 Once the lines are fused into position, stitch them down by hand or machine in the usual way (see page 5); I tend to use my usual small machine zigzag. (When you're using fusible bias you can stitch down one side of the line and then up the other if you want; because the binding is narrow, and stuck in position, it won't distort.) Carry on adding lines of binding in the order shown in the stitching sequence until the design is complete (**e**); keep any straight lines as straight as possible, and any curved sections evenly curved.

e

If any lines need corners or points, fold the binding crisply just as you do for ordinary bias binding (see page 6); press the point to hold it, then continue as usual. Once all the binding is in position, you can add extra quilting to the design if you wish, or simply finish off the design as specified in the particular project.

Making your own ...
If you want a fusible binding in a particular colour or finish and can't get hold of what you're looking for, you could always make your own. This isn't as tricky as it might sound: many quilt suppliers now sell bonding web in thin strips for precisely this purpose.

Some firms even produce gadgets that help you to make your own binding and add a fusible strip to the back as you go. Do ensure that your binding is slightly wider than the fusible strip, otherwise you'll get little bits of bonding web sticking out from the edge of the binding, which can make quite a mess when you come to iron it in place.

Extra ideas
There are various other ways in which you can use the fusible binding. Try applying it with a fancy machine stitch (**a** and **b**), or with a hand embroidery stitch (**c**, **d**). Variegated bias binding is a wonderful invention, but it can be a challenge to know what thread to use; invisible thread is a good choice here (**e**) – or use a variegated machine thread and enjoy the serendipitous colour combinations (**f**).

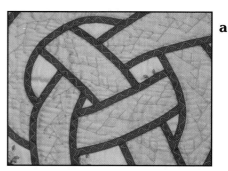

a

b

c

d

e

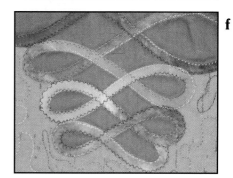

f

Four Seasons Wall-Hanging

Finished size:
10 x 58in
(25 x 147cm)
Easiness rating:
pretty easy

*C*ELEBRATE the seasons with this unusual wall-hanging made up of four mini-quilts. Each 'quiltlet' features the same leaf design in a different seasonal colourway, edged with a different colour of fusible bias binding; it's a great project for using up lots of those little scraps of fabric from your stash!

I've given requirements for the colours I've used in my sample, but feel free to vary the colours as you fancy – for instance, you might want to use yellows and  pinks for spring, or green-and-red Christmas prints on a cream-and-gold background for winter. Make sure that you choose very different colours for each season, though, so that each panel looks different.

Cotton fabrics will be best for the border rectangles, but you can use any firm fabrics (cotton, silk dupion, firm satin, bonded metallics etc) for the backgrounds and leaves. The stained glass patchwork designs can be stitched by hand or machine, whichever you prefer (although machine stitching will of course be much quicker); you'll need a sewing machine for making up the finished hanging.

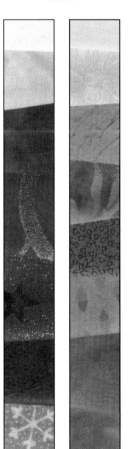

These are the fabrics I chose for my four panels: clockwise from top left, spring, summer, autumn, winter

You will need:

➤ as well as the materials listed below you'll also need a soft pencil (not a propelling pencil) and ruler; paper scissors; and 3yd (3m) of cream ribbon, ½in (12mm) wide.

Spring

➤ pale green, blue or yellow background fabric, at least 9 x 13in (23 x 33cm)

➤ toning background fabric (eg a slightly different or slightly darker colour, or a subtle pattern) 10 x 8in (25 x 20cm)

➤ five different yellow/green leaf fabrics, each 5 x 3in (13 x 8cm)

➤ two 11 x 14in (28 x 36cm) rectangles of patterned border fabric (pick one that tones well with your leaf and background fabrics)

➤ compressed polyester wadding 11 x 14in (28 x 36cm)

➤ 2½yd (2.5m) fusible gold bias binding and matching thread

Summer

➤ mid blue, green or yellow background fabric, at least 9 x 13in (23 x 33cm)

➤ toning background fabric 10 x 8in (25 x 20cm)

➤ five different bright green leaf fabrics, each 5 x 3in (13 x 8cm)

➤ two 11 x 14in (28 x 36cm) rectangles of patterned border fabric (pick one that tones well with your leaf and background fabrics)

➤ compressed polyester wadding 11 x 14in (28 x 36cm)

➤ 2½yd (2.5m) fusible green bias binding and matching thread

Autumn

➤ pale yellow, cream or peach background fabric, at least 9 x 13in (23 x 33cm)

➤ toning background fabric 10 x 8in (25 x 20cm)

➤ five different orange/yellow/ochre/tan leaf fabrics, each 5 x 3in (13 x 8cm)

➤ two 11 x 14in (28 x 36cm) rectangles of patterned border fabric (pick one that tones well with your leaf and background fabrics)

➤ compressed polyester wadding 11 x 14in (28 x 36cm)

➤ 2½yd (2.5m) fusible brown bias binding and matching thread

Winter

➤ white or pale blue background fabric, at least 9 x 13in (23 x 33cm)

➤ toning background fabric 10 x 8in (25 x 20cm)

➤ five different blue and silver leaf fabrics, each 5 x 3in (13 x 8cm)

➤ two 11 x 14in (28 x 36cm) rectangles of patterned border fabric (pick one that tones well with your leaf and background fabrics)

➤ compressed polyester wadding 11 x 14in (28 x 36cm)

➤ 2½yd (2.5m) fusible silver bias binding and matching thread

Instructions

1 Trace or photocopy two copies of the template on page 87.

2 Each of the four panels is made in exactly the same way. Begin by laying the pale background rectangle right side up over the design so that there is an even border of fabric all the way around. Trace the design in soft pencil, then use a pale crayon to draw in the letters A, B and C and the leaf numbers 1-5 (**a**).

3 Cut up the second copy of the design to give you three background templates (A-C) and five leaf templates (1-5). The other parts of the design can be thrown away. Use the templates right side up on the right side of the fabric, and cut a scant 1mm outside the edge to give you a tiny overlap when the patches are all pinned in position. Use the lettered templates to cut three shapes from the second background fabric; use the numbered templates in the same way to cut one patch from each leaf fabric. Pin all these patches in position on the background rectangle, then secure the patches in place with a small zigzag stitch (**b**).

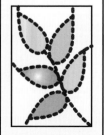

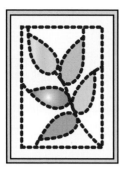

c
d

4 Lay one rectangle of border fabric right side up on a flat surface and position the design, right side up, on top, aligning the raw edges. Stitch a line of small zigzag on the rectangular pencil line around the design (**c**). Carefully cut the excess background fabric away from the edges of the design to reveal the border fabric (**d**); on the reverse of the work, carefully cut the excess border fabric away from behind the design.

5 Lay the rectangle of wadding on a flat surface and cover it with the design, right side up. Follow the sequence of diagrams shown in **e** to add the lines of bias binding, stitching them in place by hand or machine.

e

6 Put the completed design and the second rectangle of border fabric right sides together and stitch a ½in (12mm) seam all around the raw edges, leaving about 4in (10cm) open for turning (**f**). Trim the wadding back to the seam line and clip the corners; turn the design

f

right side out and press the very edges of the design to set the seams and press the seam allowances in position on the turning. Stitch the opening closed using ladder stitch. Work a line of straight machine stitching just outside the frame of binding to hold the layers together.

7 Make up the remaining three quiltlets in exactly the same way, using the appropriate fabrics and binding for each season.

8 Cut the length of ribbon in half; fold over and stitch a 3in (8cm) loop at one end of each piece, and turn under and stitch ½in (12mm) at the other end. Lay the strips of ribbon out a flat surface, with a 6½in (16cm) gap between them; a cutting board works well for this stage, as it's marked with measurements and straight lines. Pin the quilted panels in place in your chosen order, with a gap of about 1in (2.5cm) between the panels, then stitch them to the ribbon strips (**g**); I did this by slipstitching the edges of the ribbon to the backs of the panels.

g

TIP

When you're working with metallic bias binding, choose a cotton thread that matches the binding in tone and colour – this is easier than using a metallic thread, which can tend to shred. Once the binding is stitched on, it will be impossible to see that you haven't used a metallic thread.

Penguin Orchestra

Finished size:
23 x 17in
(58 x 43cm)

Easiness rating:
medium – this is a
small project, but
there are quite a few
little patches

Subtly different black
fabrics for the penguins are
set off by contrasting fabric
for the feet, and bright
ribbons for the bow ties

A ROW of penguin musicians *waits for the conductor's baton in this whimsical wall-hanging. Black fusible binding is used to edge the penguins' bodies; the triangle is created in the silver version of the binding, and the trombone is edged with the gold.*

Once all the appliqué is done, the members of the orchestra are ready for embellishing with bow ties, buttons and beads; this is an ideal way of using up all those oddments in your button box, and those little scraps of ribbon that are too short for anything else! Because of the way this design is created, it's not suitable for hand stitching; you'll need a sewing machine with a zigzag foot.

You will need:

➤ cotton fabrics as follows:

- white background fabric 23 x 17in (58 x 43cm)

- black backing/binding fabric 26 x 20in (66 x 51cm)

- two different black-and-white print fabrics for the borders:

    two strips 23 x 2in (58 x 5cm) for the top and bottom border

    two strips 17 x 2in (43 x 5cm) for the side borders

- wood-effect or brown mottled fabric for the violin 8 x 3in (20 x 8cm)

- yellow fabric for the feet 9 x 4in (23 x 10cm)

➤ black fabric(s) for the penguins. You can either use the same fabric for all the penguins (in which case you'll need one piece of fabric 21 x 13in/53 x 33cm), or you can use four very different black fabrics as I've done (in which case you'll need a 13 x 7in/33 x 18cm piece of each).

A perky bow tie adds the perfect finishing touch to each musician

For either option you can use any firm black fabric such as cotton, silk dupion, satin, velvet, brocade etc.

➤ 7yd (7m) fusible black bias binding, ¼in wide when folded

➤ 22in (55cm) fusible gold bias binding, ¼in wide

➤ 9in (22cm) fusible silver bias binding, ¼in wide

➤ silver fabric for the flute 8 x 1in (20 x 2.5cm)

➤ scrap of gold fabric for the trombone

➤ black, grey and cream sewing threads

➤ four small round silver beads for the eyes

➤ 2½yd (2.5m) silver ribbon, ⅓-½in wide, for the borders

➤ four 15in (40cm) lengths of ribbon in different bright colours, ½in wide

➤ several selections of little buttons or beads in colours to tone with the bow ties, plus – if you fancy – four small brown buttons or beads for the top of the violin, and a couple of silver ones to go on the flute

➤ compressed polyester wadding 23 x 17in (58 x 43cm)

➤ ruler, soft pencil, clear tape

Instructions

1 Photocopy the two halves of the template on pages 88 and 89, enlarging each section by 141% (A4 to A3). Stick the two photocopies together so that the lines join accurately (**a**). Lay the white fabric over the full-size drawing so that there's an even border of fabric round the main design, and pin into place. Trace all the lines and numbers in pencil, and unpin.

2 If you're using the same black fabric for all your penguins, lay it right side up under the design so that it covers all the numbered areas and pin into place. Thread your sewing machine with white and set it to a small zigzag (about 1.5 length and width); stitch along the pencil line round the edges of the four numbered sections as shown in **b**. (If you're using four different black fabrics, decide which one you're using for which penguin, then stitch them into place and cut them back individually.)

3 With small, sharp-pointed scissors, and cutting just inside the lines of zigzag, carefully cut away the white fabric from the numbered areas to reveal the black fabric underneath (**c**). When you've done this, trim away any excess black fabric from the back of the design, cutting just outside the lines of stitching.

4 Use exactly the same technique to attach the piece of wood fabric for the violin, the small gold patch at the end of the trombone, and the yellow sections for the feet (**d**). Trace the sections of the flute onto a piece of scrap paper and use these as templates to cut shapes from the silver fabric; pin these in position on the design.

5 Lay the wadding on a flat surface and position the design on top, right side up; pin the two layers together. Fuse pieces of silver bias binding in place to create the triangle and its stick; fold under the raw edge at the top of the stick to neaten it. Stitch these bits into place with a small zigzag in grey thread (**e**).

6 Follow the sequence shown in **f** to add the pieces of gold fusible binding to create the trombone.

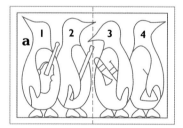

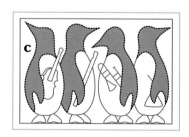

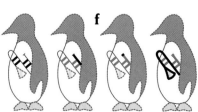

Position and stitch the four straight brace pieces first, then the section leading to the mouthpiece, then add a short straight section for the mouthpiece itself, turning under the raw edges. Finally, fuse the long piece in position round the main section of the trombone, but don't stitch this down yet.

7 Follow the sequence shown in **g** to add the lines of black bias binding; adding them in this order ensures that all the raw ends of binding are covered. Stitch the lines marked on each diagram in place before you move onto the next diagram. When you come to lines going into the edges of the trombone and the flute, tuck the raw ends of the black binding under the metallic bias binding. Once all the black binding is stitched in place, stitch the edges of the flute and the remaining section of the trombone.

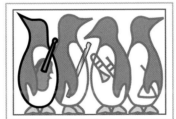

g

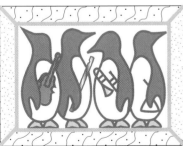

h

8 Cut the border shapes from the full-size drawing and use these as templates to cut two side strips and two top and bottom strips from the black-and-white print fabrics. Position these on the design and pin, then cover the diagonal joins with silver ribbon. Stitch these strips into place, then add a frame of silver ribbon round the inner edge of the border (**h**).

9 Use your machine to stitch four strings (lines of straight stitch) and a base-line (satin stitch) onto the violin.

10 Lay the backing fabric right side down on a flat surface and position the design on top of it, right side up, so that there's an even border of black fabric all the way around. Fold the raw edges over the front of the design in a small double hem and stitch in place by hand or machine (**i**).

i

11 Stitch the silver beads in position to create eyes. Fold each piece of ribbon into a double fold (**j**) then wrap the end round the centre a couple of times to create a bow; cut off any excess and stitch the raw end firmly at the back to anchor the bow. Stitch a bow tie onto each penguin and add toning buttons down each one's shirt front (**k**).

j

12 If you wish, add four extra brown buttons or beads on the neck of the violin and a couple of silver ones to the flute. Add a small casing to the back, loops along the top edge or a couple of curtain hooks for hanging the panel.

k

TIP

Using white thread in your sewing machine for appliquéing the black fabrics means that you can see the stitching more easily on the wrong side; this makes it easier to trim the excess black fabric away from the stitching.

Taming Challenging Fabrics

ONE of the (many!) wonderful things about stained glass patchwork is that you can use virtually any kind of fabric for the patches – and, if you wish, you can mix and match the fabrics within a project. Silks, metallics, shiny satins, textured polyesters, lace: they all look wonderful incorporated into stained glass patchwork, as you can see from the projects in this section. Some fabrics do present particular challenges, though, and it's worth knowing some tips to help you get the very best out of them.

Silks

Silk fabrics work wonderfully with stained glass patchwork; the sheen on the fabrics makes them glow when they're outlined with bias binding. I've experimented with various kinds of silk, and I've found that dupion works best; it's firmer and slightly thicker than some other woven silks, and it's not too sheer. Like most other silk fabrics, though, it does fray badly, so I've developed a way of using it in SGP that minimises the problem of fraying. This is a technique which you can use for other slippery fabrics such as satin, too; it also works well for very large projects, when you don't want the entire piece covered with pins but don't want to have to tack all the patches

1 Draw out your full-size pattern and cut it up to use as templates in the usual way. Pin the template onto the silk just as you usually do, but instead of

cutting the silk exactly along the edge of the template, add a couple of mm – maybe a very scant quarter of an inch – outside

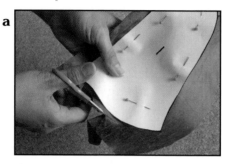

the template (**a**). You don't need to be exact; you're not actually adding a seam allowance, you're just giving yourself a little overlap.

2 Once you've cut out all the patches, lay them on the wadding or foundation fabric; you'll find that the patches all overlap each other slightly (**b**).

Fidget them around so that the patches and the overlaps look even; if you have a choice, lay a darker fabric over any lighter ones to avoid darker fabrics showing through on the surface.

3 Once all the patches are in the right place, pin them in position, then set your sewing machine to a medium-width zigzag and stitch along the raw edges between the patches. Begin with the T-junctions, then

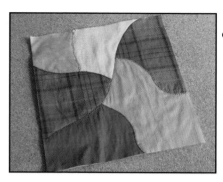

work your way through the longer lines (**c**). This stitching secures the raw edges and stops them from fraying while you're working; it also means that the patches can't slowly fray and pull out from under the binding after the piece is completed. An extra bonus is that the zigzagging holds all the patches in place while you add the binding. Once all the patches are secure, you can go on and add the bias binding just as usual (**d**).

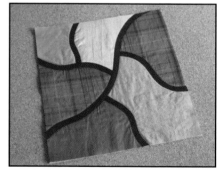

Metallics

I love using glitzy metallic fabrics – and these look particularly spectacular when they're combined with SGP. There are all kinds of fabulous metallic fabrics available these days, and happily many quilt suppliers are stocking them, so if you've been dying to try them, now's the time to branch out! Many people are wary of using metallic fabrics, though, because they seem so very different from using cottons. Won't they melt and stick to the iron? Don't they fray terribly? It's true that metallic fabrics do behave a bit differently from cottons, but once you understand the different types and the ways in which you can get the best out of them, they're as easy to work with as cottons.

As you explore the world of metallic fabrics, you'll find many other types that don't fit into the categories I've talked about below; just cut little samples and experiment with them till you've found the best way of working with that particular fabric. And if you're doing a whole project in metallic fabrics, you might find it helpful to use the same method that I use for working with silk; cut all the patches a little bit bigger than the templates, and zigzag them all in place on a foundation fabric before you begin adding the binding.

• Cottons decorated with a metallic print (**a**) can be treated just the same way as ordinary cottons. You'll find that you can

press them, cut them, piece them and quilt them just as you do classic cotton patchwork fabrics. The same is true of cotton/metallic lamés (**b**), which are cottons woven with a smattering of metallic threads.

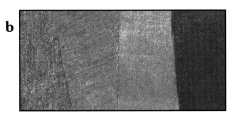

• Bonded metallic fabrics (**c**) are my favourites, because they're very easy to use and very good-natured. They don't fray, and many of them can be ironed on either the right side or the wrong side – do try a tiny sample out first, though, because they do vary in this! They're available in many different colours, including variegated shades, prints and holographic effects. Some of the bonded metallics are a bit stretchy, as they're manufactured for things like swimsuits and dance costumes; if the one you want to use is a bit floppy, use spray starch to give it some body. Lay the fabric face down on the ironing board, cover it with a fine spray of starch, and iron the starch dry. The fabric's now much more stable, which makes it easier to cut your patches.

Some of the bonded metallics have a surface almost like foil (**d**); if you pin through them the pins can leave permanent little holes. This is easily got round, though; just make sure that you pin any patterns on at the very edges, where any stray holes will be covered later by the bias binding, and do the same when you're pinning the patches onto the backing.

• A few years ago the only metallic fabrics easily available were the loosely-woven lamés (**e**). The big problem with lamés is that they fray very badly; I still use them in

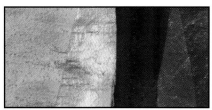

my work, because they come in a wonderful range of colours, but I get over the fraying problem by backing the lamé with lightweight iron-on interfacing. Cut a piece of interfacing slightly smaller than the fabric piece, lay the fabric right side down on the ironing board, and lay the interfacing glue side down on top. Fuse the interfacing in place (**f**); this gives the fabric extra body as well as helping it not to fray, and you can then cut your patch and pin it onto the backing in the usual way.

• Some metallic fabrics are covered in shaped and coloured sequins (**g**) – and if you've ever accidentally put an iron on a sequin, you'll know straight away what the challenge is with using fabrics like these ones!

The sequins melt, come unstuck and move off their backing, – and, just for good measure, the backing melts and distorts too. So, if you're going to use this kind of fabric successfully, you need a thick protective layer between the fabric and the iron. Use

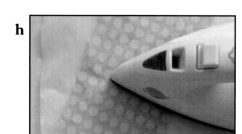

h

a Teflon sheet (**h**), iron the fabric from the back wherever possible, and use the lowest heat for the shortest time that's practical. If you treat these fabrics very gently, you can still incorporate them into your designs; I've used several sequinned fabrics in the *Church Window* design on page 51.

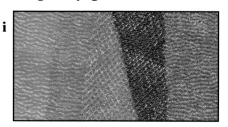

i

• Sheer or lacy metallic fabrics (**i**) present the same challenges as using ordinary lace. Overcome this problem by layering them with another fabric; pin the two layers together, and either cut your patch out from the double fabric, or zigzag round the shape of the patch and then cut out the shape just outside the stitching line. As you add the bias binding around the shape, the two layers will be secured together.

Synthetics and other slippery customers ...

• Some synthetic fabrics (**a**) are firm, closely-woven and stable, and don't need any special handling at all; I've used lots of fabrics like this in stained glass patchwork projects, treating them just the same way as cottons.

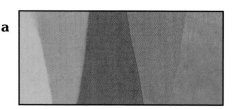

a

• Fabrics such as velvets, corduroys, fur fabrics and thick laces (**b**) have a pile or heavy texture; if you put a hot iron

b

straight onto the right side of fabrics like this, you can flatten the texture and spoil the look of the fabric. Instead, keep a little towel folded up by your ironing board and lay the fabric right side down on the towel and press from the back (**c**). The soft

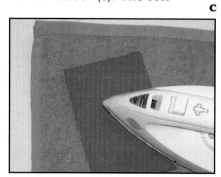

c

towelling cushions and protects the pile or the texture of the fabric so that you can press it without spoiling it.

• Occasionally fabrics have a lovely pattern but are too sheer (**d**) to use just as they are for

d

stained glass patchwork; when I'm using fabrics like this, I give them extra body by adding a layer of lightweight iron-on interfacing (see the lamé section above).

• Some heavy woven fabrics fray badly, but if they're already quite thick you don't want to add any thickness by using interfacing. One way to reduce the fraying problem is to work a stabilising

line of stitching round the edges of the patch. Draw round the template with a soft pencil, then use your machine to work a line of small zigzag round the drawn shape; cut out the shape, slightly outside the stitching, and the patch is ready to use (**e**).

e

• Nets and laces (**f**) often have attractive patterns woven into them, but they are too sheer to use as they are in SGP because they show too much of the background. Follow the instructions I've given above for lacy metallic fabrics to layer them up with firmer fabrics.

f

• Satins have a beautiful sheen which I like exploiting in SGP. If you've ever tried using satin, though, you'll know that it's *very* slippery. This can make it tricky to cut accurate patches, but you can make the fabric more stable by spraying the back with spray starch and then ironing it dry. The heat dries the starch and sets it at the same time, giving you a much more stable fabric which you can then cut more accurately with scissors or rotary cutter. Do try the starch out on a small sample first, though; on a few fabrics it might leave a slight watermark – in which case you could try backing the satin with iron-on interfacing instead.

Tulips

Finished size:
22 x 17in (56 x 43cm)
Easiness rating:
medium

Real and imitation silk
dupions in soft colours
combine well in this design

*C*HARLES *Rennie Mackintosh is particularly well-known for his rose designs, and these in turn have inspired many quilters and other artists (see page 68!) Less well-known are his other flower designs; my inspiration for this exotic wall-hanging came from Mackintosh's fabric patterns featuring stylised tulips. I created the design in a mixture of real and imitation silks, using soft pastels enhanced by the subtle tones of the silver fusible binding.*

You will need:

➤ silk dupion (or equivalent) as follows:
- mid purple for the backing/binding 24 x 19in (61 x 48cm)
- pale blue background 22 x 17in (56 x 43cm)
- mid blue border 22 x 17in (56 x 43cm)
- pale dusky pink for the stems 20 x 14in (50 x 36cm)
- creamy yellow for the flower heads 16 x 8in (40 x 20cm)
- pale sage green for the main leaves 17in (43cm) square

- mid sage green for the leaf details 13 x 9in (33 x 23cm)
- mid purple for the oval details 9 x 6in (23 x 15cm)
- pale purple for the larger ovals 8 x 2in (20 x 5cm)
- ➤ compressed wadding 22 x 17in (56 x 43cm)
- ➤ 9yd (9m) fusible silver bias binding, ¼in (6mm) wide
- ➤ white or grey sewing thread
- ➤ soft pencil, paper, felt pen, clear tape

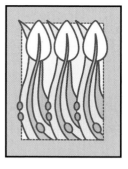

d   e

Instructions

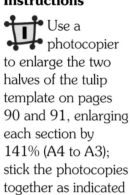
a

1 Use a photocopier to enlarge the two halves of the tulip template on pages 90 and 91, enlarging each section by 141% (A4 to A3); stick the photocopies together as indicated with clear tape (**a**). Go over the lines with felt pen to make them darker. Lay the pale aqua/blue background fabric right side up over the design; pin in place, then trace all the outlines of the design with soft pencil (**b**).

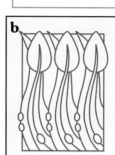
b

2 Cut the flower, leaf and oval shapes out of the paper template (the rest of the template can be discarded), then use these to cut shapes from the appropriate fabrics; remember to use the templates right side up on the right sides of your fabrics. Pin the fabric shapes in position on the traced design (**c**), and secure with a small zigzag.

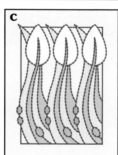
c

3 Lay the blue border fabric right side up on a flat surface and position the design, right side up, on top, aligning the raw edges. Stitch a line of small zigzag around the silhouette of the design – that is, round the marked rectangle and any areas that jut out into

the border (**d**). Carefully cut the excess background fabric away from the edges of the design to reveal the border fabric (**e**); on the reverse of the work, carefully cut the excess border fabric away from behind the design.

4 Lay the wadding on a flat surface and position the design, right side up, on top, aligning the raw edges; secure the layers together using your favourite method – tacking, tack gun, quilt glue, safety pins etc. Follow the sequence shown in **f** to add the lines of bias binding. Where there's an asterisk on the diagram, leave a small edge of the binding line unstitched, as you'll have to tuck the end of a binding line underneath at a later stage.

5 Lay the backing fabric right side down on a flat surface and position the design on top of it, right side up, so that there's an even border of backing fabric all the way around (**g**). Fold the raw edges over the front of the design in a small double hem and stitch in place by hand or machine (**h**). Add a small casing to the back or loops along the top edge for hanging the panel.

g

f
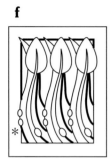

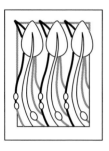

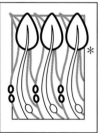

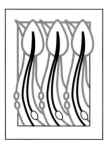

Church Window

Finished size:
42in (107cm) square
Easiness rating:
challenging

*N*OT surprisingly, church window designs provide wonderful sources of inspiration for stained glass patchwork. This particular design is an amalgam of several ancient window patterns, and the gold binding and shiny fabrics add to the slightly ecclesiastical feel. I've used all kinds of different exotic fabrics for my patches – plain and figured silks, velvets, satins, shiny polyesters, sequinned fabrics, brocades, and various kinds of metallic fabric. Because lots of them are slippery, it's worth stitching them in position even if they don't fray; this makes it easier to add the binding without the patches moving out of place.

Some of the exotic fabrics
I used for the window
design

You will need:

➤ exotic fabrics in a range of toning colours, about 2m in total to give you plenty of choice; as a guide, I used about 20 different fabrics, but you could use fewer (or more!)

➤ foundation fabric 40in (102cm) square

➤ compressed wadding 42in (107cm) square

➤ backing/binding fabric 46in (117cm) square

➤ 16yd (15m) ribbon, ½in (12mm) wide (you'll need more if you want to subdivide some of the patches)

➤ 13yd (12m) gold bias binding, ½in (12mm) wide when folded

➤ cream/yellow sewing thread

➤ quilting threads to match the colours of your patches

➤ assorted gold beads for embellishment (optional)

➤ soft pencil, paper, felt pen

Instructions

Enlarge the templates on pages 92-94 by 141% (A4 to A3). Cut the templates out, and use them as guides for cutting the fabric shapes as follows:

    use template A to cut four shapes

    use template B to cut four shapes

    use template C to cut four shapes

    use template D to cut sixteen shapes (eight of these go on the outer parts of the large curved rosette, eight on the inner sections)

    use template E to cut four shapes

    use template F to cut four shapes

    use template G to cut eight shapes (four of them as mirror-images)

    use template H to cut eight shapes (four of them as mirror-images)

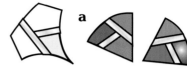 I decided to sub-cut the large shapes (A, D and E) into different sections then re-assemble them into the shapes with straight lines of ribbon (**a**); if you prefer to keep things simpler, you can miss out this stage!

3 Position all the pieces on the background fabric (**b**), following the layout shown (**c**), and secure them with a medium zigzag.

b

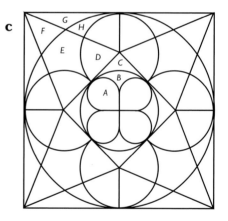

c

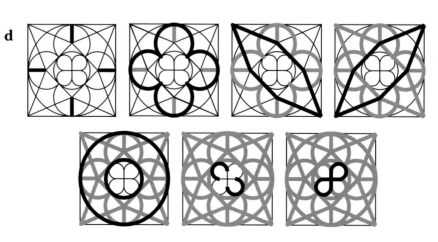

d

4 Lay the wadding on a flat surface and position the design right side up on top, with an even border of wadding all round; secure the layers together using your favourite method – tacking, tack gun, quilt glue, safety pins etc. Follow the sequence shown in **d** to add the lines of ribbon and bias binding, stitching by hand or machine.

5 Lay the backing fabric right side down on a flat surface and position the design on top of it, right side up, so that there's an even border of fabric all the way around (**e**).

Fold the raw edges over the front of the design and stitch on a frame of ribbon to cover the raw edges (**f**). Quilt round each patch, working about ¼in (6mm) inside the lines of gold ribbon or binding, then scatter beads in various parts of the design if you wish. Add a small casing to the back or loops along the top edge for hanging the panel.

f

e

TIP

Ribbon is fine for the straight lines of the design – in fact, it works better than bias binding on these lines as it isn't constantly trying to curve. You'll probably find that it's cheaper than bias binding, too.

The detail shows some of the D shapes which I've subdivided into separate patches with straight lines of ribbon. Beads are scattered across different parts of the design in a random arrangement. I've quilted the design by stitching around each individual patch.

Iris Landscape

Finished size:
40 x 24in
(102 x 61cm)

Easiness rating:
challenging; there are lots of pieces in the design and lots of lines of bias binding

*A*S someone who's always enjoyed ordinary stained glass as well as the stitched version, I've always loved the work of Louis Comfort Tiffany – the man who gave his name to what we now call Tiffany lamps. Like all the other Art Nouveau designers Tiffany loved exotic flora and fauna: butterflies, dragonflies, lilies, peacocks etc – and he also created many designs featuring irises. This tranquil landscape was stitched as a commission for my friend Diane Vellacott, but she was happy to let me include it in the book, so that you can have the chance to stitch your own version. To capture the exotic feel that Tiffany got in his glass pieces, I've used a very wide variety of fabrics including silks, metallics, synthetics, batiks and some overprinted cottons.

You will need:

➤ fabrics as follows:

- subtle print cotton border fabric 40 x 24in (102 x 61cm)
- toning backing/binding fabric 42 x 26in (107 x 72cm)
- white cotton foundation fabric 40 x 24in (102 x 61cm)
- assorted pale blue 'sky' fabrics (you'll need roughly ½yd/50cm in total)
- assorted mid green 'hill' fabrics (you'll need roughly ½yd/50cm in total)
- assorted pale aqua 'water' fabrics (you'll need roughly a long ¼yd/25cm in total)
- large scraps of 8-10 different purple/blue fabrics for the flowers
- long scraps of 3-4 different bright green fabrics for the leaves

➤ compressed polyester wadding 38 x 26in (96 x 66cm)

➤ 18yd (18m) black bias binding, ¼in (6mm) wide

➤ 12in (30cm) square of tear-away foundation paper, or A4 sheet of cartridge paper

➤ black sewing thread and machine embroidery thread

➤ machine quilting threads for the sky, hills and water

➤ soft pencil, paper, felt pen

Instructions

1 Use the grid method (see page 10) to enlarge the design on page 95; go over the lines with felt pen to make them darker. Lay the white foundation fabric right side up over the design; pin in place, then trace all the outlines of the design with soft pencil (**a**).

2 You'll find it easiest if you work through the large parts of the design first, then, the smaller parts. Cut out all the sky pieces from the paper design, then use these to cut shapes from the appropriate fabrics; remember to use the templates right side up on the right

sides of your fabrics. Pin the fabric shapes in position on the traced design (**b**), and secure with a small zigzag. Do the same with the pieces for the hills and the water (**c**).

3 Now cut and assemble the flowers and leaves, one bloom at a time; cut out the fabric patches and pin them in position, then secure them with a small zigzag. The central part of the design is now complete (**d**).

4 Lay the print border fabric right side up on a flat surface and position the design, right side up, on top, aligning the raw edges. Stitch a line of small zigzag around the silhouette of the design – that is, round the marked rectangle and any areas that jut out into the border (**e**). Carefully cut the excess background fabric away from the edges of the design to reveal the border fabric (**f**); on the reverse of the work, carefully cut the excess border fabric away from behind the design.

Some of the exotic fabrics I used for the iris design

a

b

c

d

e

f

5 Lay the wadding on a flat surface and position the design, right side up, on top, aligning the raw edges; secure the layers together using your favourite method – tacking, tack gun, quilt glue, safety pins etc. Add lines of free machine quilting across the sky (**g**), working across

g

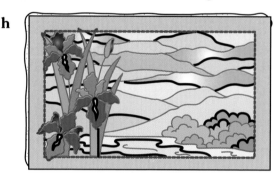

all the sky sections; then work lines on the hills to echo the outlines, and wiggly lines on the water.

6 It's now time to add the lines of bias binding; working your way through the T-junctions (see page 4), add the lines of binding until the design is complete. To start you off, I've indicated the first lines to be added in diagram **h**.

h

7 Once all the binding is in position, thread your machine with the machine embroidery thread and set it up for satin stitch or close zigzag (see page 64 for hints on this). Stitch decorative details on the hills and water where they're indicated on the pattern (**i**).

i

Remember to use a piece of foundation paper under the stitching, then tear away the excess once you've finished stitching.

8 Lay the backing fabric right side down on a flat surface and position the design on top of it, right side up, so that there's an even border of fabric all the way around (**j**). Fold the raw edges over the front of the design in a small double hem and stitch in place by hand or machine (**k**). Add a small casing to the back or loops along the top edge for hanging the panel.

j

k

TIP

Quilting the extra lines on the design before you add the binding means that you can work long lines across the sky and hills if you wish without the stitching showing on the black binding.

Crazy Techniques

JUST as the name suggests, these are a mixture of ordinary stained glass patchwork and crazy patchwork. I came up with idea because I love the effect of crazy patchwork, but I get bored with turning all the edges under, and I don't like the slightly lumpy effect you sometimes get when the edges are turned; on the other hand, I don't like the way the fabrics fray when you *don't* turn them under …

I was puzzling over this one day, and it suddenly occurred to me: why couldn't I do crazy patchwork by using stained glass patchwork – covering the raw edges of the fabric with straight lines of binding or ribbon, which I could then also decorate with embroidery or other fancy embellishments if I wanted? I tried a few samples out, and I was soon hooked. Try it out yourself – maybe you'll become hooked too!

Usually stained glass patchwork uses bias binding for creating the lines of the designs, but of course you only need to use bias binding when the design has curves in it. If your design is completely made up of straight lines, there are all kind of alternatives you can use. This is your chance to try out ribbons, braids, strips of fabric, seam binding tape, petersham, broderie anglaise, lace (see the examples on page 10) – anything that will create an attractive line. Varying the different bindings and colours you use adds to the 'crazy' – that is, the random – effect of the finished piece (**a**).

a

You can combine ribbons and braids in one strip; if you want to use a translucent ribbon or a piece of lace, layer it over a ribbon or tape in a more solid colour to create a composite strip (**b**). You can also stitch on the strips of various ribbons and braids and then embellish them with machine or hand embroidery, beadwork etc. Try adding lines of embroidery stitches along the stained glass leading strips (**c**); herringbone, single and double feather stitch, fern stitch, chain stitch and Cretan stitch all work well. If your machine does attractive automatic stitches, you can also decorate your binding strips that way (**d**).

In this section you'll find two projects that I've created using crazy stained glass patchwork; you'll probably think of many more ideas. If you want to add a really Victorian touch to your work once you've finished adding the bindings, decorate some of the fabric panels with beaded or embroidered motifs.

b

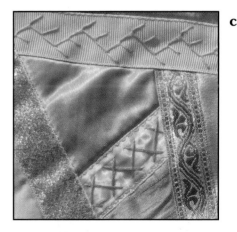

c

d

Crazy Cushion Covers

Easiness rating:
pretty easy; the
patchwork is
straightforward,
though you might
want to spend a bit
of time adding extra
embellishment

Bright silk dupions and
toning ribbons make for an
exotic-looking cushion

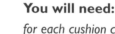

*T*HE *gorgeous sheen of silk dupion lends itself wonderfully to these exotic cushion covers, created in crazy stained glass patchwork. I've used exactly the same patches for each cover, using wide ribbons decorated with hand embroidery, but their finished appearance is quite different.*

The slightly more restrained one uses black for the ribbon and the embroidery, creating a subtle texture; the second version is much more over-the-top, featuring ribbons in various colours and contrasting embroidery decorated with beadwork. Of course the covers can be created using any fabrics; if you have cottons left over from making curtains or other cushions, make some extra covers to tone in with your own decor.

You will need:

for each cushion cover

➤ 18in (45cm) square of white foundation fabric

➤ 18in (45cm) square of compressed wadding

➤ two 18 x 10in (45 x 25cm) rectangles of backing fabric

➤ large patches of bright silk dupion in various colours

➤ roughly 3yd (3m) ribbon, either all one colour or assorted, 1in (25mm) wide; the exact amount will depend on how many patches you divide your square into

➤ sewing thread to match the ribbon(s) and the backing fabric

➤ hand embroidery threads and/or beads for embellishing (optional)

➤ 18in (45cm) square of plain paper

➤ pencil, long ruler, felt pen, pale crayon

Instructions

1 Using the long ruler and pencil, draw straight lines to divide the piece of paper into random patches; begin by drawing a diagonal line randomly across the whole area, then draw other lines at different angles (**a**). Starting with one long line helps to

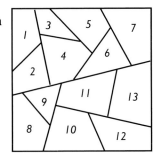

create a more balanced final design. Number the patches, then go over the lines with felt pen to make them stronger.

2 Lay the foundation square over the drawing and trace the straight lines in pencil; draw in the numbers using pale crayon (**b**). Cut up the paper pattern (take a copy of it first if you might want to use the same design again), and use these shapes as templates to cut your fabric patches; remember to use the templates right side up on the right sides of your fabrics. Pin the patches in position on

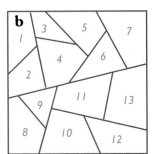

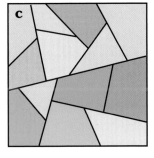

the foundation square (**c**); if you're using silk or any other fabric that frays badly, secure the patches with a medium zigzag.

3 Lay the wadding on a flat surface and position the design on top, right side up; secure the layers using your favourite method. Add the lines of ribbon, beginning with the T-junctions as usual (see page 4), and stitching either by hand or machine. I've drawn the sequence of adding lines for the design I used (**d**), but your design might require a different order.

d

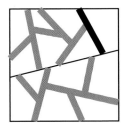
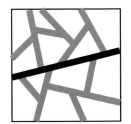

4 If you wish, embellish the lines of ribbon with hand or machine embroidery stitches, and/or beading. If you want to add beads, avoid the final inch (2.5cm) of each line of ribbon, so that they don't get in the way of the machine when you're making up the cushion cover.

5 Trim the quilted design to ensure that the edges are even and the corners square. Fold under and stitch a small double hem on one long edge of each backing rectangle (**e**). Lay the quilted design right side up, then position the backing pieces on top, right sides down, aligning the raw edges so that the backing pieces overlap (**f**).

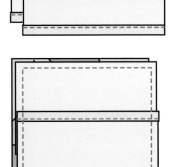

Stitch a ½in (12mm) seam all the way around, then trim the wadding back to the seam line and clip the corners. Turn the cushion-cover right side out, and press just the very edges to set the seams.

TIP

Don't worry if your first experiment with creating the design doesn't balance very well; simply rub out the lines and have another go. Or use a fresh square of paper!

Herb Cushion

Finished size:
14in (36cm) square
Easiness rating:
pretty easy

Some of the exotic fabrics and braids I used for the herb cushion

YOU can go really over the top with this design, embellishing it to your heart's content with beads, ribbons, pearls and hand embroidery. The silk dupion embroidered with rosebuds that I used for the background square was a piece I fell in love with even though it was very expensive; happily, the design looks just as good with ordinary dupion or satin!

The basic design is a simple New York Beauty block; here I've developed the basic technique of working with block designs (see page 28), adding plenty of exotic fabrics and trimmings. And don't feel that you have to stick to the colourscheme I've used; this design would look wonderful in rich, royal colours embellished with gold or silver.

You will need:

➤ two 15in (38cm) squares of cream silk dupion

➤ embellished cream silk or other embroidered fabric 10in (25cm) square

➤ sage green silk 6in (15cm) square

➤ thick cream lace 4in (10cm) square

➤ cream brocade fabric 9in (23cm) square

➤ pale sage green fabric 6 x 4in (15 x 10cm)

➤ 50in (125cm) mid sage green ribbon, ½in (12mm) wide

➤ 2yd (2m) assorted ribbons, lace, tape, braid etc in toning colours

➤ stranded embroidery thread, coton à broder etc in toning colours

➤ assorted beads, buttons, pearls, readymade appliqué motifs, ribbon roses etc

➤ cream sewing thread and others to match your ribbons and beads

➤ synthetic stuffing and a small amount of pot pourri, dried lavender or dried herbs

Instructions

1 Trace or photocopy the templates A-D on page 96. Cut these out, and use them as templates to cut shapes from the fabrics as follows (remember to cut the shapes slightly bigger so that they don't fray too much):

  using template A, cut one shape from the cream lace

  using templates A and B combined (so that you have a complete quarter-circle), cut one shape from the the sage green silk

  using template C, cut one shape from the cream brocade fabric

  using template D, cut three shapes from the pale sage green fabric

2 Pin the sage green quarter-circle into one corner of the embroidered silk square and pin the lace shape on top (**a**). Add the curved shape of cream brocade fabric, then position the three pale green triangles on top (**b**) and pin in place.

3 Lay the square of wadding on a flat surface and cover it with one of the squares of plain dupion. Position the decorated square on top, making sure that there's an even border of fabric all the way around (**c**). Secure all the shapes to the background with a medium zigzag.

4 Add lines of your chosen ribbon or tape to the edges of the triangular shapes (**d**), and stitch in place by hand or machine. Then cover the three curved lines with different ribbons or braids (**e**). Cover the edges of the embroidered square with green ribbon (**f**), keeping the lines straight and the corners crisp.

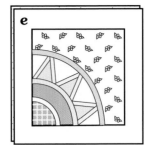

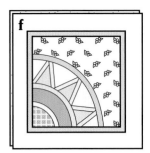

5 Embellish the design with hand or machine embroidery and quilting, beads, motifs, ribbon roses etc as you wish. (If you want to add quite large beads near the edges of the design, as I've done on the centres of the border, you'll find it easiest to do these after you've made the cushion up, so that they don't get in the way of your machine stitching.)

6 Put the design and the remaining square of silk right sides together, and stitch a ½in (12mm) seam all the way around the square, leaving roughly 6in (15cm) open for turning (**g**). Trim the wadding to the seam line, clip the corners and turn the design right side out; fill softly with the stuffing, slipping the pot pourri, lavender or herbs into the centre of the stuffing. Close the turning with ladder stitch.

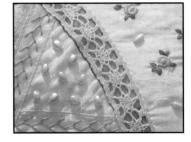

I used pearl beads to embellish and quilt the design at the same time

a

b

In this detail you can see the ruched ribbon, the upholstery braid, and little seeding stitches I've used to embellish the patch of green silk.

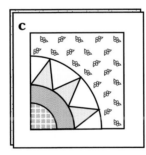

c

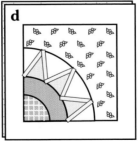

d

TIP

Remember that you'll need braids or lace with some 'give' to go around the curves in step 4; loosely-woven upholstery braids work well, and also have interesting textures. For the middle curve I used an ordinary ribbon, which I ruched up by running gathering threads along the edges.

Stained Glass Stitchery

A few years ago, I was pondering how to create an SGP design with more detail in it. When you're using bias binding to surround lots of small patches of fabric, if you're not careful you can end up with more binding than fabric, so I was trying to work out a way around this. I came up with the idea of using lines of black machine satin-stitch instead of bias binding, which I realised would give me greater freedom and flexibility in the designs I stitched, so I got to work trying the idea out. It worked wonderfully; I call this technique stained glass stitchery, to distinguish it from 'proper' stained glass patchwork using binding.

The two projects in this section use stained glass stitchery in slightly different ways, but both of them make use of a strong line of contrasting satin stitch to outline shaped patches. Within the instructions for the projects themselves you'll find more hints and tips for creating a really handsome satin stitch.

Sunflower Bowl

*L*IKE many other people, I was very taken with Linda Johansen's books on making bowls and boxes out of stiffened fabric. With this design I've taken her basic idea a few steps further, creating the flower-shaped bowl out of individual petals. Each part of the design is edged with a contrasting line of satin stitch, which serves to neaten the shapes as well as decorate them. The fabric patches are stiffened with a material called Timtex, which is available from many quilt suppliers; you could also experiment with other stiffening agents such as firm Vilene and buckram.

For visual interest, use a mixture of plains (solids) and mottled fabrics or small prints; I chose a brown batik fabric for the centre of the flower

You will need:

➤ nine different yellow fabrics, two 3 x 4in (8 x 10cm) patches of each

➤ two 5in (13cm) squares of brown cotton fabric

➤ nine Timtex patches 3 x 4in (8 x 10cm)

➤ one 5in (13cm) square Timtex patch

➤ eighteen 3 x 4in (8 x 10cm) patches of double-sided bonding web

➤ two 5in (13cm) squares of double-sided bonding web

➤ large reel of dark brown sewing thread

➤ soft pencil, thin card, stick glue, paper scissors

Instructions

1 Trace or photocopy the sunflower bowl templates A and B on page 85. Stick the shapes onto the card and cut them out (**a**).

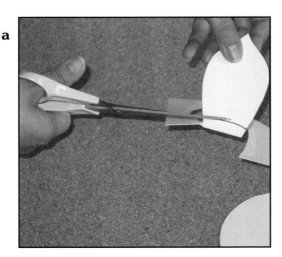

a

2 Lay a patch of yellow fabric *wrong side up* on your ironing board and position one of the small patches of bonding web on top, web (rough) side down. Fuse the web on with a warm iron (**b**). Do the same with all the patches of yellow fabric.

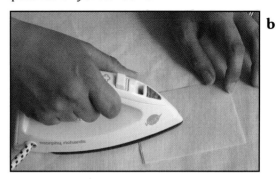

b

3 Peel the paper way from the back of one yellow patch to reveal the bonding web; lay this web (rough) side down on one small Timtex shape, and fuse into place (**c**). Fuse the matching piece of yellow fabric to the other side of the Timtex shape in the same way. Cover all the smaller Timtex shapes in this way.

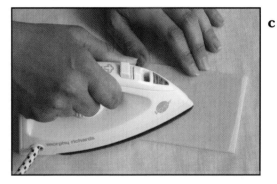

c

4 Lay the petal template A on one side of a covered patch and draw round the shape in pencil; cut the petal shape out (**d**). Draw and cut out the other eight petals in the same way.

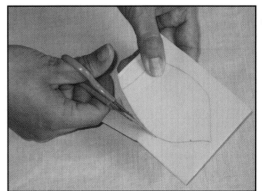

d

5. Follow the same method to cover the Timtex square with brown fabric; use template B to cut the circle for the base of the bowl.

6. Set your sewing machine up for satin stitch and thread it with brown thread.

There are several tips which will help you to get a really good, even satin stitch out of your sewing machine. First of all, look on your bobbin case – the bit that holds the bobbin in the machine. If the arm of your bobbin case has a tiny hole in it, thread the bobbin thread through that hole before you put the case in the machine; this helps to keep the bobbin thread at the back of the work and stops it coming to the surface and making the edge of your satin stitch look slightly ragged. If your bobbin case hasn't got one of these holes, don't worry; you should still be able to do a passable satin stitch!

I'm very fond of rayon machine-stitching thread for doing satin stitch, which is very fine and gives a lovely smooth finish to the stitch, but you can use ordinary cotton thread if you prefer; just set the stitches very slightly further apart if you're using a thicker thread.

g

e

Work a neat satin stitch up one side of each petal and down the other (**e**); don't stitch across the bottom edge of the petal at this stage. Stitch all the petals in the same way.

f

7. Arrange the petals regularly around the circular base and secure in position with a small zigzag stitch (**f**). Now set the machine back to satin stitch and work a neat circle of stitching all round the circumference of the base (**g**).

8. Set the machine back to a small zigzag. Pull each pair of petals gently together (**h**) and stitch from the base upwards for about 1in (2.5cm). The stitching will be camouflaged against the satin stitch. Stitch each pair of petals together for the same distance; the longer your lines of stitching, the steeper the sides of the bowl will be. Your bowl is now ready for use.

h

TIP
Don't worry too much about the tips of the petals, if it's difficult to make the satin stitch look neat right at the top; you can always add a yellow or brown bead to each petal tip to disguise any slight irregularities!

Poppies Picture

Finished size:
14 x 10½in
(36 x 27cm)

Easiness rating:
fairly complicated

*P*OPPIES *are perennial favourites. This little picture perfectly captures their striking colourscheme of scarlet petals, emerald leaves and rich black centres, enhanced by the lines of black machine satin stitch edging each patch. The patches are appliquéd in place first with zigzag; this stitching stops the patches from fraying, and also shows you where to work the satin stitch. If you're slightly hesitant about trying a design with so many different patches, try the simpler version described in the tip box.*

You will need:

➤ cotton fabrics as follows:
- firm cream background fabric 13 x 10in (33 x 26cm)
- five or six different mottled/batik red fabrics, 6in (15cm) square of each
- mottled grey/black for the flower centre 3 x 2in (8 x 5cm)
- green 'grass' fabric for the border 14 x 10½in (36 x 27cm)
- two different greens for the leaves, 7in (18cm) square of each

➤ tear-away foundation fabric 13 x 10in (33 x 26cm) (or an A4 sheet of cartridge paper)

➤ black machine embroidery thread

Mottled and batik reds help create a dramatic design

Instructions

1 The trick with this version of stained glass stitchery is that the appliqué is actually stitched from the back of the work, so the first thing you'll need is a reverse version of your full-size drawing. One of the best ways of doing this uses a photocopy of the design (see page 97). While the photocopy is still fairly fresh, lay it face down on the wrong side of the cream background fabric and press it firmly with a hot iron. The lines should transfer onto the fabric, giving you a reverse image. If the lines are a bit faint, go over them with a soft pencil to fill in any gaps.

If it's not practical for you to use a photocopier, trace the design on page 97; go over the lines with felt pen to make sure that they're nice and dark. Lay the design face down on a lightbox and trace it onto the back of your foundation fabric; if you don't have a lightbox, tape it to a window on a sunny day. (If you don't have a sunny day … think about moving to California?)

2 Remember that the drawing becomes *the back* of your work, so any fabric must be added to *the front*. This seems slightly complicated at first, but you soon get into the swing of it. If it helps, write BACK in large letters on the frame of your design, where it will be covered by the border fabric!

3 Decide which of the red fabrics you'd like to go where on the design. Choose one of the large petals to begin with, and cut a patch of the appropriate red fabric comfortably larger than the petal shape. Remember that this needs to go on *the front* of the work, so position the fabric patch on the front of

the cream fabric, hold it up to the light to check that the fabric goes over the whole area of the petal with good margins round the edges, and then pin it in place (**a**).

4 Set your machine to a small zigzag – about 1.5 width and 1.5 length, the same kind of size we use for stitching on bias binding – and then stitch along all the lines that border that particular petal (**b**).

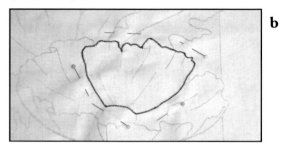

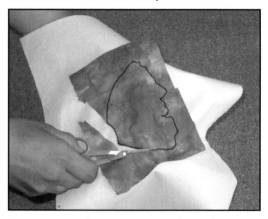
b

5 Now you need to trim off the excess fabric around the petal shape on the front of the design. Use a small pair of sharp-pointed scissors for this, and carefully cut away the spare fabric *outside* the stitching lines (**c**) – not inside; that's the bit you need!

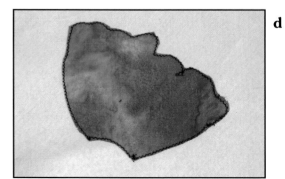
c

Trim pretty close to the stitches; if you accidentally snip one or two it's not the end of the world, as the stitching will all be covered by satin stitch later on. Here's how the design looks with all the excess red fabric trimmed away (**d**).

a
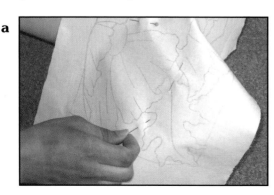

d

6 Continue adding the petal shapes in the same way, stitching and trimming each one individually, until all the petal patches are in position (**e**).

e

7 Use exactly the same technique to add the two parts of each leaf shape and the black patch in the centre of the large poppy (**f**). Add the border in

f

the same way (remember this time to cut away the excess fabric *inside* the line of stitching, not outside), and then stitch lines of straight stitch along all the little detail lines on the design (**g**).

g

8 Set your machine up for a medium-width satin stitch (see page 64 for hints) and position the piece of tear-away foundation fabric (or cartridge paper) behind the design. From this stage onwards you're going to be stitching on the *front* of the work. Now you have to pay attention to the T-junctions (see page 4), just as when you're adding bias binding, because you're

going to be neatening off the ends of the lines of machine stitching by covering them with later ones, just as we neaten off raw ends of bias binding.

Beginning with the first T-junctions (the centre-lines of the leaves are a good place to start), work satin stitch over each of the lines of black stitching. Use medium-width stitching over the main parts of the line (**h**), tapering the stitch gradually when you're working on a line that ends in a point. Use a slightly narrower satin stitch, tapering at

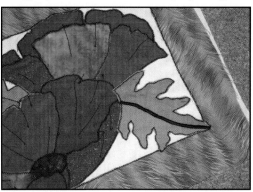

h

the ends, for the isolated lines. If you find that your work is puckering slightly, stretch it in a small embroidery/quilting hoop suitable for using under your machine.

9 Once you've covered all the lines with satin stitch, the final stage is to remove the foundation fabric from the back of the work; you do this simply by carefully tearing it away from the stitching. If your work has pulled out of shape at all (sometimes all the satin stitch can cause a bit of undulation), spray it with cold water and pin it out flat and square on a clean surface – for instance a pinboard covered with sheeting. Spray it with a little spray starch too, if you like. Once it's dry, it will be nice and flat and ready to frame.

TIP

If you'd like to try a much simpler version of the design first, use the same red fabric for all the petals; you can stitch round the outlines of both flowers as one large patch, and simply work lines of straight stitch to mark the edges of the different petals. If you do try this version, though, use a batik or random-dyed red fabric so that different tones show in various parts of the flowers.

Fused Techniques

THIS technique is a bit different from other ways of doing stained glass patchwork. By cutting shapes out of a single piece of black (or other dark-coloured) fabric, you still get the contrast between the black outlines and the bright patches, but you can create dark areas that are uneven in shape and width. You could, of course, neaten the raw edges of the black fabric with needle-turning or satin stitch, but a much quicker method is to use either double-sided bonding web, or iron-on interfacing. Once the fabric design is assembled you can then quilt it by hand or machine; the rose picture in this section is machine-quilted, while the jungle wall-hanging makes use of big-stitch hand quilting.

Art Nouveau Rose

Finished size:
roughly 9 x 12in
(23 x 30cm)
Easiness rating:
easy

THE Glasgow designer Charles Rennie Mackintosh worked in stained glass as well as many other disciplines, and his favourite motif was the stylised rose. I've created several stained glass patchwork designs inspired by his work, and here's another little one; a simple rose picture, created by cutting back through black fabric to reveal coloured patches. Pick batik or marbled fabrics or ones with tiny allover prints or textures; they give the finished picture more interest than plain solids.

You will need:

➤ cotton fabrics as follows:
- black for the background 10 x 14in (25 x 36cm)
- red/pink fabric for the rose 10 x 14in (25 x 36cm)
- gold for the border 10 x 6in (25 x 15cm)
- green for the leaves 8 x 4in (20 x 10cm)

➤ double-sided bonding web 10 x 14in (25 x 36cm)

➤ compressed wadding 10 x 14in (25 x 36cm)

➤ black machine-quilting thread

➤ pencil

➤ picture-frame with an aperture to fit the design (roughly 9 x 12in/23 x 30cm)

Batik and mottled fabrics provide visual interest across the design

a

Instructions

1 Lay the bonding web paper (smooth) side up over the pattern on page 98 and trace the lines in pencil (**a**). Lay the black fabric right side down on an ironing board and position the bonding web design web (rough) side down on top; fuse it into place with a warm iron (**b**).

b

2 Using small, sharp-pointed scissors carefully cut all the shapes out of the black fabric (**c**).

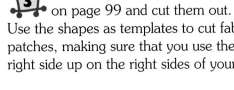

c

3 Trace or photocopy the shapes on page 99 and cut them out. Use the shapes as templates to cut fabric patches, making sure that you use them right side up on the right sides of your

fabrics. Cut templates A and B from the gold fabric, and templates C and D from the green fabric.

4 Position the fabric patches, right sides up, in the appropriate places underneath the black frame and pin (**d**). Lay the red/pink fabric right side up on a flat surface and position the black frame on top, aligning the raw edges (**e**). Press the design carefully with an iron to fuse the layers together (**f**), removing the pins as each piece is fused.

5 Lay the wadding on a flat surface and cover with the design, aligning the raw edges. Pin together in a couple of places, then work free machine quilting around and between the coloured patches, working on the black fabric (**g**).

6 Trim the design as necessary to fit into the frame. If your frame comes with a glass front, you may prefer to remove the glass so that you can see the quilted texture better.

d

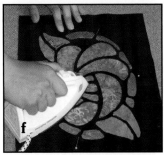
e

f

g

TIP

If you're using a fabric that frays badly for your coloured patches, such as silk dupion or satin, stabilise it first by fusing lightweight iron-on interfacing on the back.

It's a Jungle Out There...

Finished size:
40 x 28in
(102 x 70cm)

Easiness rating:
medium – the
technique itself is
easy, but the quilt is
quite large

This design uses only two
fabrics; choose two that
have a good strong tonal
contrast

*T**HIS** way of creating a stained-glass-type design could hardly be easier; the dark silhouette is one piece of fabric, fused to the bright background fabric with double-sided bonding web so that the edges don't fray. Pick a cheerful fabric for the background to create the impression of looking out from a dark jungle to a sunlit clearing. You'll need to buy the interfacing off the roll; the packs are much too small.*

You will need:

➤ 1yd (1m) dark green mottled cotton fabric

➤ 1yd (1m) bright jungle/animal cotton print

➤ backing fabric 40 x 28in (102 x 70cm)

➤ medium-weight iron-on interfacing 40 x 28in (102 x 70cm)

➤ compressed wadding 40 x 28in (102 x 70cm)

➤ large skein of variegated green coton perlé

➤ large skein of multicoloured coton perlé

➤ pencil

Instructions

1 Use the grid method (see page 10) to enlarge the design on page 100; go over the lines with felt pen to make them darker. Lay the piece of iron-on interfacing right (smooth) side up over the drawing; pin the two together, then trace all the lines of the design in pencil (**a**).

2 Press the dark green fabric and lay it out on a flat surface, *wrong side up*. Lay the interfacing, glue (rough) side down, on top; put a few pins in to keep the web in position, but don't use too many as they will get in the way of the iron. Working from one short side slowly down the design, press the back of the interfacing with a warm iron to fuse it in place (**b**).

3 Using small, sharp-pointed scissors, carefully cut away all the fabric and interfacing from the central area and all the other *spaces* between the different parts of the design (**c**).

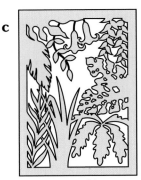
wrong side

right side

c

4 Press the bright print fabric and cut a 40 x 28in (102 x 70cm) rectangle from it. Lay this rectangle out on a flat surface, *right side up*. Lay the cut-out design *right side up* on the top of the multicoloured fabric (**d**); pat the shape carefully into place so that the raw edges of both fabrics align – the bonded shape will have a tendency to distort slightly as you've now cut the centre out. Once you're happy with its position, pin the design in place then run a few lines of large tacking stitches round the edges of the dark design and down the centres of the stems and large leaves (**e**).

d   **e**

5 Lay the backing fabric right side down on a flat surface and cover it with the wadding. Position the tacked design on top, right side up, and secure the layers together using your favourite method – tacking, tack gun, quilt glue, safety pins etc. Beginning at the centre of the design and working outwards, work a line of big-stitch quilting just outside the green silhouette, using the multicoloured coton perlé. Once this is done, work a similar line just inside the green silhouette, using the variegated green thread (**f**); if you wish, you can create the effect of the fern fronds weaving under and over each other.

f

6 Cut 2in (5cm) strips from the remaining bright or dark fabric – whichever you prefer – and use them to bind first the sides and then the top and bottom of the quilt. Make a hanging casing and hand-stitch it to the back of the quilt top.

TIP

The fabric requirements I've given for the bright print are for an allover (non-directional) design. If the fabric you want to use has a definite direction, check which way it's printed; you might need a 40in (102cm) length rather than just a yard/metre, so that you can cut the panel in the correct orientation.

Foundation Piecing

FOUNDATION piecing is one of the techniques that's revolutionised quilting over the last few years – it's a superb way of achieving straight lines and crisp points without having to worry about exact seam widths (something close to my heart …!), and the results are all but miraculous. It's also another rather intriguing way of building up stained glass patchwork designs that consist of straight lines. Some quilters use foundation piecing for designs that need even-width strips of 'leading' fabric between the patches; I've never quite seen the point of that, as I find it easier to create such designs using tape or ribbon (see page 28). I do think it's very effective, though, for creating slightly quirky designs that feature lines of uneven widths.

As you'll already know if you're a fan of foundation piecing, this is another technique worked on the back of the project. You can stitch on a paper pattern, which is torn away once the stitching is complete, but I find that the relatively narrow leading strips between the coloured patches make it easier to work on firm interfacing, which doesn't need to be removed afterwards.

Christmas Tree

Finished size:
10½ x 13½in
(27 x 34cm)

Easiness rating:
pretty easy
(especially if you're
used to foundation
piecing)

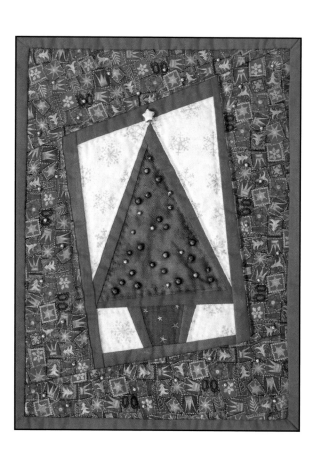

IF (like me) you find it difficult to create pieced blocks that are even and symmetrical, try this technique: make the design deliberately wonky! The folksy feel of this Christmas tree is created by the angles and varying widths of the 'leading' lines; for this design I've worked the lines between the patches in blue, which produces a good contrast with the patches without being too dominating. Once your design is complete you can decorate it to your heart's content with little beads, stars, sequins etc; I've also quilted round the fabric patches.

Subtle prints and plains pick up the colours of the strong border print fabric

You will need:

➤ cotton fabrics as follows:
- blue for the backing/binding 12 x 15in (30 x 380cm)
- blue for the leading lines 12in (32cm) square
- mottled or print green for the tree 7in (18cm) square
- red print for the pot 2½in (6cm) square
- cream/gold print for the background 8 x 11in (20 x 28cm)
- Christmas print for the border 16in (40cm) square

➤ compressed wadding 10½ x 13½in (27 x 34cm)
➤ interfacing fabric 10½ x 13½in (27 x 34cm)
➤ blue sewing thread
➤ quilting threads to match your fabrics
➤ assorted Christmassy beads, sequins, charms etc to decorate
➤ soft pencil, ruler, pale crayon
➤ rotary cutter, ruler and board

Instructions

1 Lay the interfacing over the template on page 101 and trace all the lines in soft pencil; use a ruler to ensure that the lines are good and straight. Add the numbers in pale crayon, as shown in **a** (don't use the pencil, in case the numbers show through any light patches).

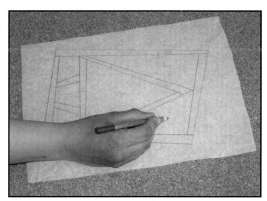

a

2 Trim the patch of red fabric roughly to shape so that it's comfortably larger all round than patch number 1 on the drawing; pin it in place on the *front* of the work (the side without the drawn lines), so that it covers the area marked 1; the back of the work will look as shown in **b**, and the patch on the front will look as shown in **c**.

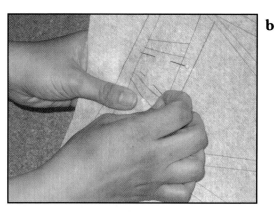

b

c

3 Cut the square of blue leading fabric into eight strips, each 1½in (4cm) wide. Cut one of these strips into half across its width and pin one piece, right side down, over the tub patch on the front of the work so that the raw edges roughly align (**d**).

d

On the back, stitch by machine along the line between patches 1 and 2 (**e**). On the front of the work, trim the raw edges to about ⅛in (2mm) beyond the seam line; fold the blue fabric strip to the right side and press it in position. Add the second short strip of blue to the other side of the pot in the same way.

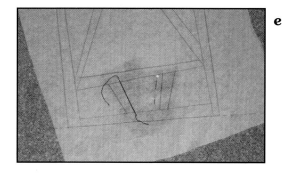

e

f

4in 4in

8in

3in

4 Cut the cream background fabric into two 4 x 11in (10 x 28cm) rectangles, then sub-cut each of these into one 4 x 3in (10 x 8cm) rectangle and one 4 x 8in (10 x 20cm) rectangle (**f**). Add the smaller patches to the sides of the pot, pinning the patches on the front of the work and stitching on the back as before (**g**).

g

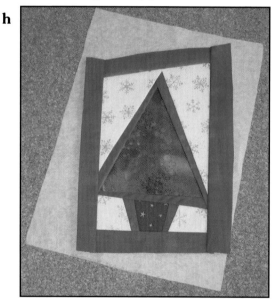

5 Continue working your way through the patches in order, using the remaining strips of blue fabric for the narrower patches, the green for the tree and the remaining cream fabric for the background (**h**).

h

i

5in 8in

6 Cut the border fabric into two 8 x 16in (20 x 40cm) rectangles, then sub-cut each of these at an angle as shown to create four asymmetric shapes (**i**). Add these to the design in the order indicated to cover the final four patches (extend your stitching lines along the dotted lines marked on the template).

j

The foundation-piecing is now complete (**j**). Check the alignment of the tree against the template on page 101, then trim the quilt to a 10½ x 13½in (27 x 34cm) rectangle.

7 Lay the wadding on a flat surface and position the design, right side up, on top; pin in a few places to hold the layers together. Quilt round each patch by hand or machine, then stitch on any embellishments you'd like to use.

8 Lay the backing fabric right side down on a flat surface and position the design on top of it, right side up, so that there's an even border of blue fabric all the way around. Fold the raw edges over the front of the design in a small double hem and stitch in place by hand or machine. Add a small casing, hanging loops or a couple of curtain hooks for hanging the panel.

> **TIP**
>
> Make sure that you're using stitch-in (rather than iron-on) interfacing, and that it's reasonably firm; the medium or heavy weights work well, but the light versions will be too floppy.

Seascape

Finished size:
25 x 10½in
(63.5 x 26.5cm)

Easiness rating:
medium – the stitching is simple, but there are quite a few patches

Pick a selection of plains and random prints for the patchwork

*T*HIS simple but very attractive seascape is an excellent way of using up lots of different fabric scraps. Don't worry if you don't have quite as many different fabrics as I've suggested (is that likely, I ask myself?); you can always use the same fabric for two or three neighbouring patches, especially if your fabrics are batiks or random prints. This design works best on sew-in interfacing, but so that you can see the lines more clearly on the step-by-step photographs I've stitched my examples onto a paper foundation.

You will need:

➤ cotton fabrics as follows:
- seven different 'sky' colours, each 8 x 4in (20 x 10cm)
- twelve different 'sea' colours, each 24 x 4in (20 x 10cm)
- printed border fabric, two 25 x 2½in (64 x 6.5cm) rectangles, two 10½ x 2½in (26.5 x 6.5cm) rectangles
- black backing/binding fabric 28 x 13½in (71 x 34cm)
- black fabric for the leading lines, one 30 x 8in (80 x 20cm) rectangle, and two 22 x 1½in (56 x 4cm) strips

➤ 2oz wadding 25 x 10½in (63.5 x 26.5cm)

➤ medium/heavy interfacing 24 x 9in (60 x 23cm)

➤ black or navy sewing thread

➤ hand quilting threads and variegated cotons à broder in green/blue colours

➤ round beads in green/blue colours and various sizes

➤ a few large shaped beads or charms (starfish, fish, shells etc)

➤ soft pencil, ruler, pale crayon, clear sticky tape

➤ rotary cutter, ruler and board

a

b

Instructions

1 Photocopy each section of the seascape template on pages 102 and 103, and stick the photocopies together with clear tape along the line indicated to create a full-size pattern (**a**). Lay the interfacing over the pattern and trace all the lines in pencil; use the pale crayon to write in the numbers. (As each patch is edged by a line of black fabric after you apply it I haven't numbered the black strips individually.)

2 To help you decide which fabric to use where, cut little patches of each sky and sea fabric and move them around on the paper design until you're happy with the arrangement. When you've decided, stick the little patches on the photocopy (**b**), then pile your sea and sky fabrics up in order with fabric number 1 on the top of the pile and fabric number 19 at the bottom.

3 Cut the 30 x 8in (80 x 20cm) rectangle of black fabric into twenty 1½ x 8in (4 x 20cm) strips.

4 Lay the patch of fabric number 1 on the right (blank) side of the interfacing and pin it in position so that it covers patch number 1 (**c**). (Remember

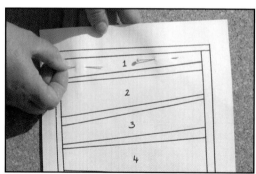

c

that I'm working on a paper pattern in the photographs, so your design will look slightly different at each stage as it's on the interfacing.) Lay one of the 8in (20cm) strips of black fabric right side down on top so that the raw edges are roughly aligned, and pin in position (**d**).

d

On the back of the work – the side with the pencil marks – stitch along the bottom edge of patch 1 (**e**).

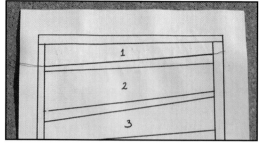

e

Turn to the front of the work again and trim the raw edges about ⅛in (2mm) away from the seam line; press the fabric strip to the right side (**f**).

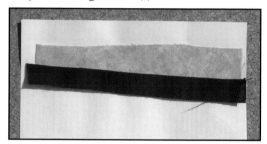

f

5 Continue adding the fabric patches and black strips alternately, working your way through the pile of sky and then sea fabrics in order, finishing with patch 19 (**g**).

6 Use the same technique to add the long black strips to the sides of the design and then finish off the top and bottom with the remaining short strips of black fabric (**h**).

g   **h**

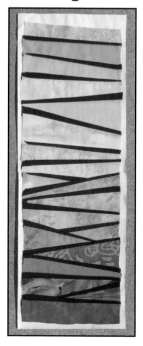

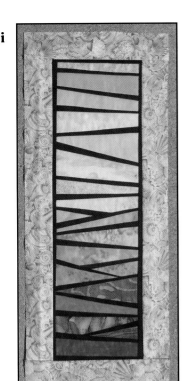

i

7 Add the long strips of border fabric to the sides of the design, then the short strips to the top and bottom (**i**). Trim the design so that the edges are straight and the corners square.

8 Lay the black backing fabric right side down on a flat surface and position the wadding on top of it so that there's an even border of black fabric all the way around. Lay the patchwork design, right side up, on top of the wadding, and secure the layers together using your favourite method. Work lines of hand or machine quilting across the sea and sky patches; I quilted the sea with lines of big-stitch quilting in coton à broder (**j**), and the sky in ordinary hand-quilting thread (**k**).

Stitch the round beads in random clusters across some of the sea patches, and stitch on the large shaped beads or charms (**l**). Finally, work a line of big-stitch quilting just outside the black strips bordering the patchwork centre.

9 Fold the raw edges over the front of the design in a small double hem and stitch in place by hand or machine. Add a small casing, hanging loops or a couple of curtain rings for hanging the seascape.

TIP

I found a lovely shell print in sea colours for my border fabric; you could use one of the pebble, sand or water prints on the market instead if you prefer.

---

j

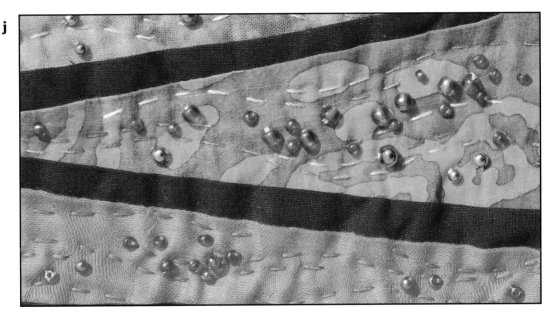

k

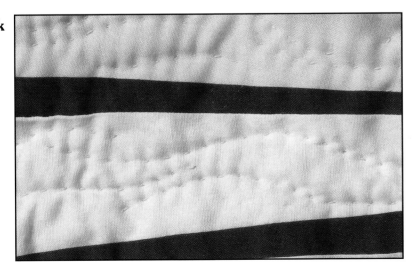

l

Trouble-Shooting

I'VE mentioned often that stained glass patchwork is a very easy, and a very forgiving, technique – and so it is. It's difficult to make a mistake that will totally spoil a SGP project, but every now and again a little section doesn't go quite the way you want it to, and when that happens it's good to know how to put it right quickly and easily.

Taken a wrong turning?

The first is when you miss a T-junction. Remember that we talked about the T-junctions when we were looking at the basic technique (see page 4); ideally you want to stitch the stem of a T first, so that you can cover the raw end of the bias binding with the cross-bar.

Well, if you do a lot of SGP, every so often you'll be pinning on a line of bias binding and you'll come to a T-junction you've missed; there's nowhere to tuck the raw end of the bias binding, because you've stitched down the line it goes into. This still happens to me now and again, even after working in this technique for years!

The way to solve this problem is the same whether you're stitching by hand or machine. Use a seam ripper to cut gently through a few stitches; once you've done this, you can slip the raw end of the bias binding underneath, then redo the stitches you unpicked.

There; that wasn't too difficult, was it? To avoid repeating the problem, look hard at your design before you begin adding the lines; if you're not sure you can remember the order for stitching on the lines, mark them 1, 2, 3 etc on your pattern.

Wandered off the straight and narrow?

Sometimes your attention can wander for a moment while you're stitching by machine, or the hand guiding the material slips fractionally. The result of this can be that you miss stitching a little section down one edge of the bias binding.

The remedy for this is similar; use a seam ripper or sharp-pointed scissors to unpick the stitches that have wandered off the edge, then re-stitch the gap to secure it. Stitching slightly more slowly might help you to avoid the problem in the future. It's also helpful to use an open-toed appliqué foot if you have one, or a clear appliqué foot; either will help you to see where you're going a bit more easily.

Threads peeping out?

Occasionally you might notice that you haven't quite caught the raw edge of the fabric underneath the stitching. This can happen with either hand or machine stitching, but the remedy is the same: again it involves unpicking the stitches next to the errant bit of fabric.

Once you've taken them out, push the fabric securely under the edge of the binding and stitch it in place. If you know there isn't a large margin of fabric underneath the binding, stitch over the area twice by machine, or make your hand-stitches very close together for extra security.

Having a bit of a stretch?

When you're stitching down both sides of a curve by machine, it's best to begin each line of stitching from the same end. If you work down one side and then up the other, you can end up with the binding pulling slightly and forming creases. Often you can cure this simply by pressing the binding with a steam iron, which will flatten out small creases. If the creases are very severe, you may need to take out one line of stitching, press the binding to remove the creases, then stitch that side of the binding again.

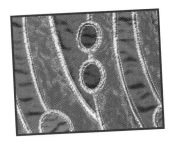

Lavender Sachets
This template is full size

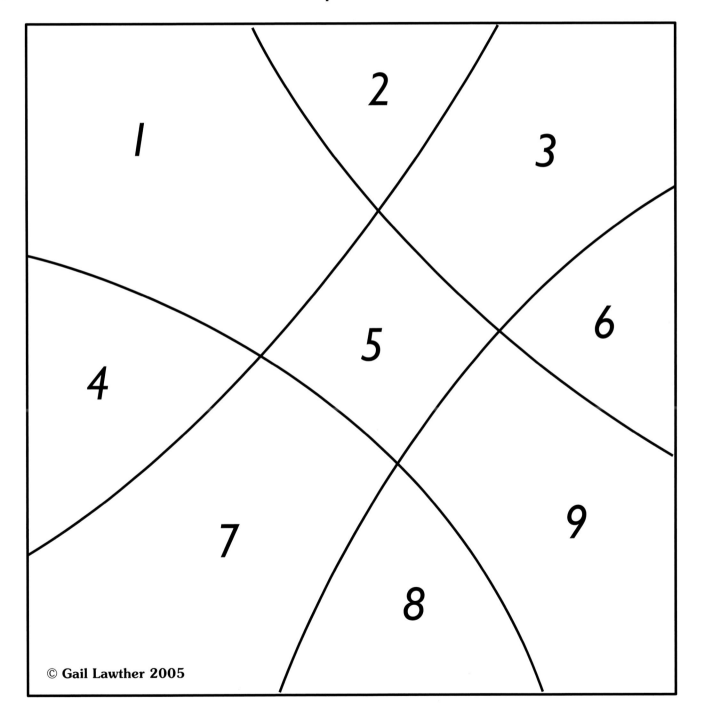

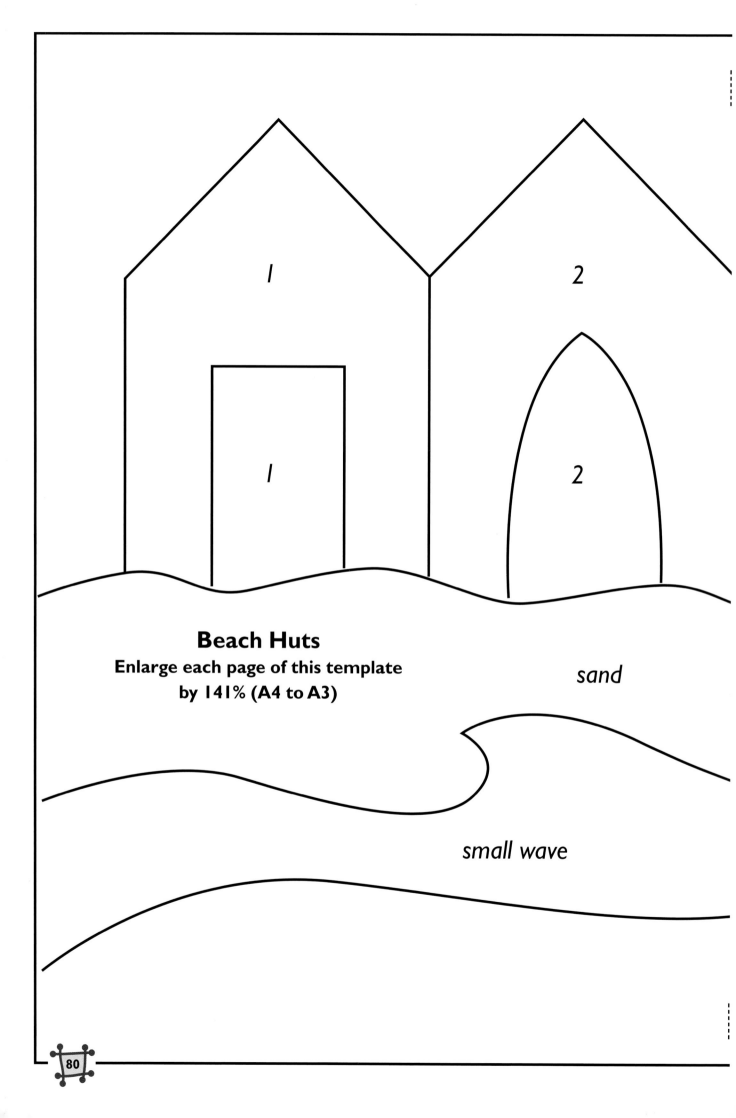

Beach Huts
**Enlarge each page of this template
by 141% (A4 to A3)**

sand

small wave

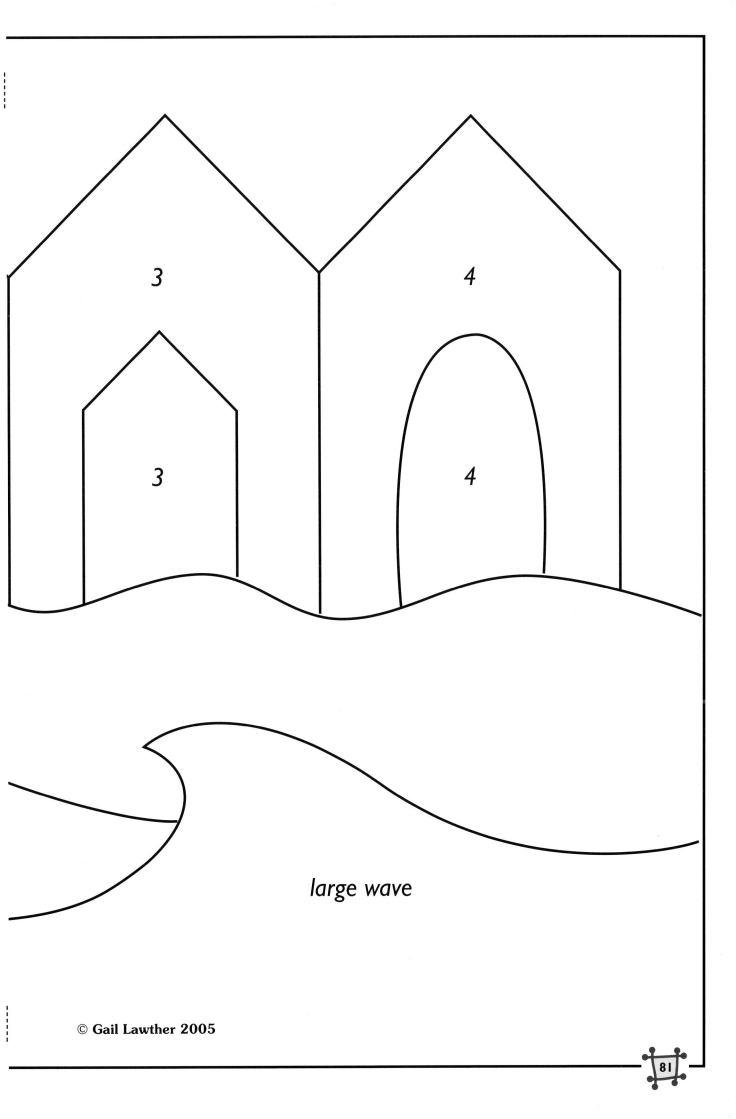

3

4

3

4

large wave

81

Bonbon Cushions

Enlarge the design so that each square measures 3in (8cm)

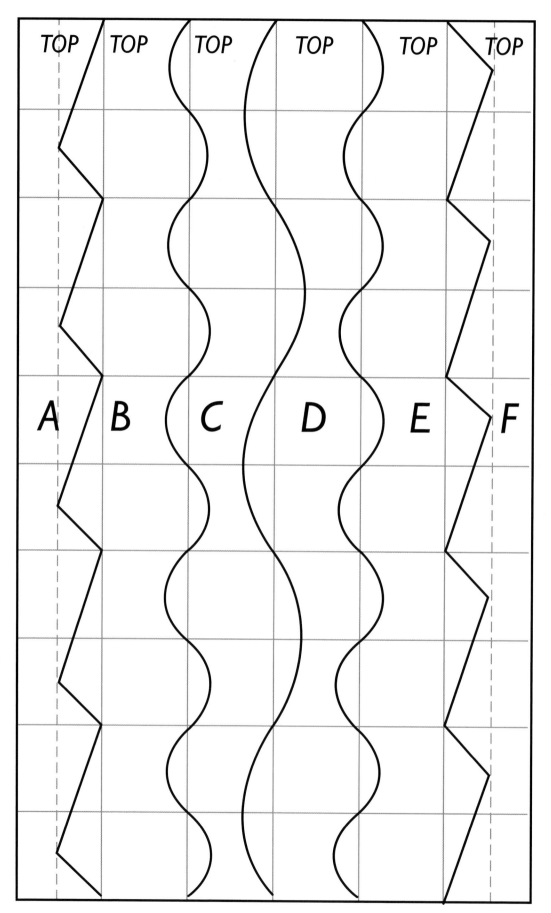

Seashells Sofa Throw

Enlarge the design so that each square measures 4in (10cm)

83

Fish Supper

Enlarge the design so that each square measures 6in (15cm)

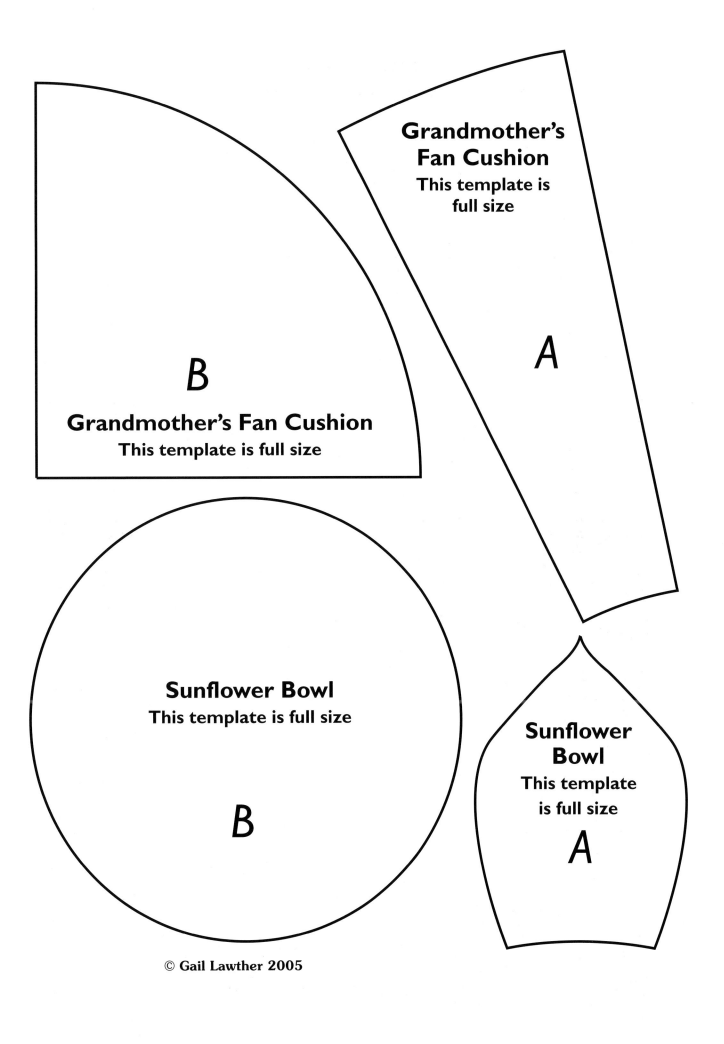

Grandmother's Fan Cushion
This template is
full size

A

B

Grandmother's Fan Cushion
This template is full size

Sunflower Bowl
This template is full size

B

Sunflower Bowl
This template
is full size

A

© Gail Lawther 2005

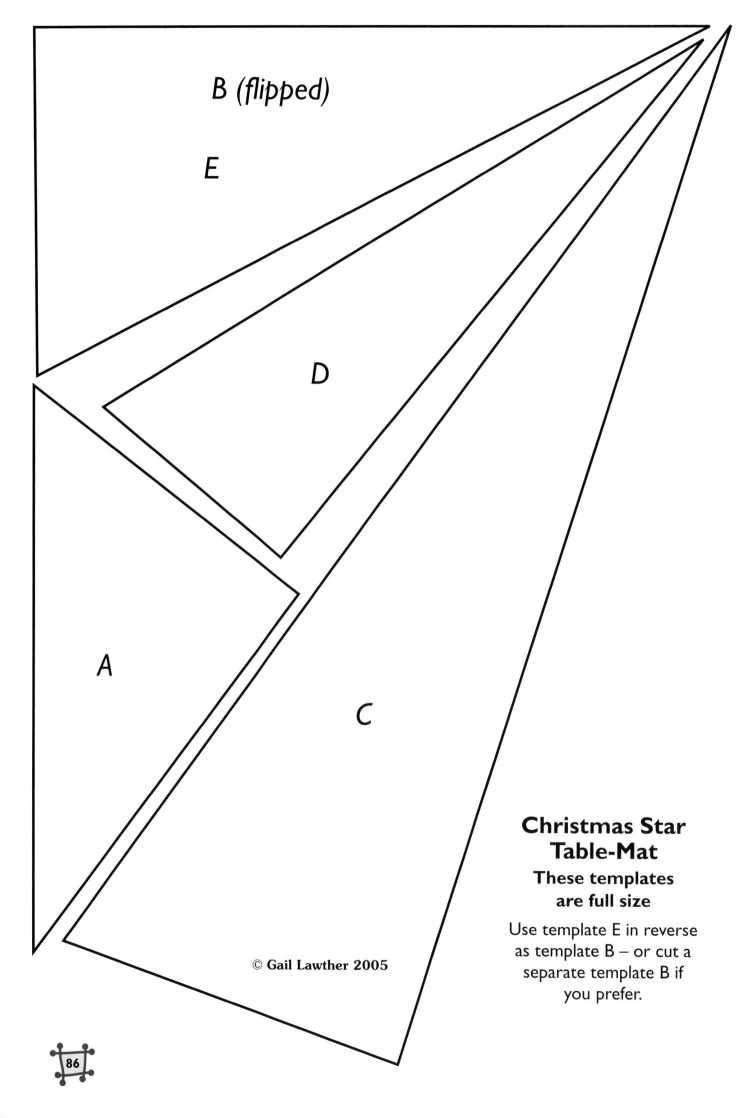

B (flipped)

E

D

A

C

**Christmas Star
Table-Mat**
**These templates
are full size**

Use template E in reverse
as template B – or cut a
separate template B if
you prefer.

© Gail Lawther 2005

Four Seasons Wall-Hanging
This template is full size

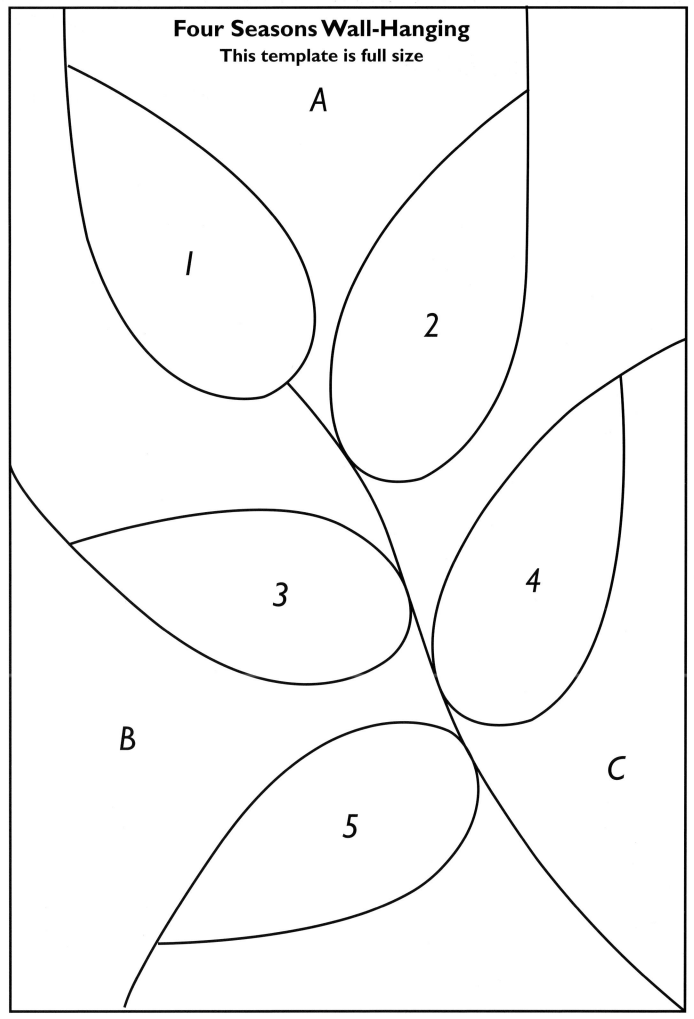

A

1

2

3

4

B

5

C

Penguin Orchestra

Enlarge each page of this template by 141% (A4 to A3)

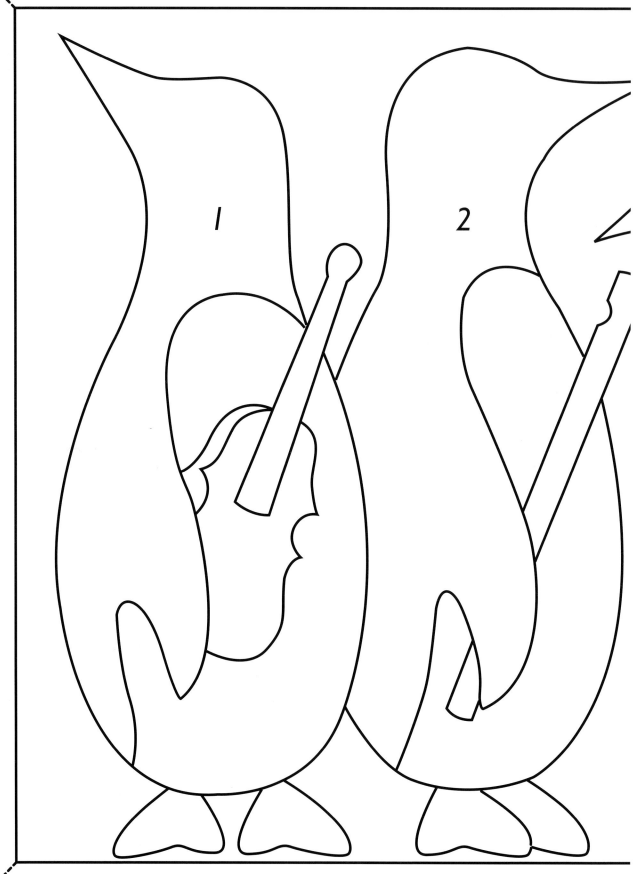

© Gail Lawther 2005

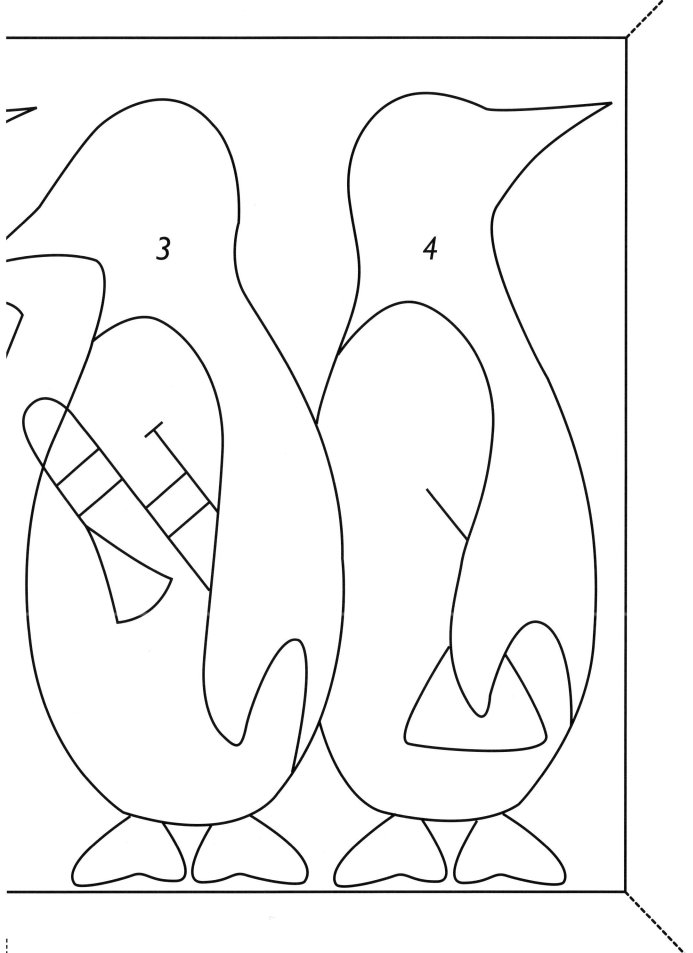

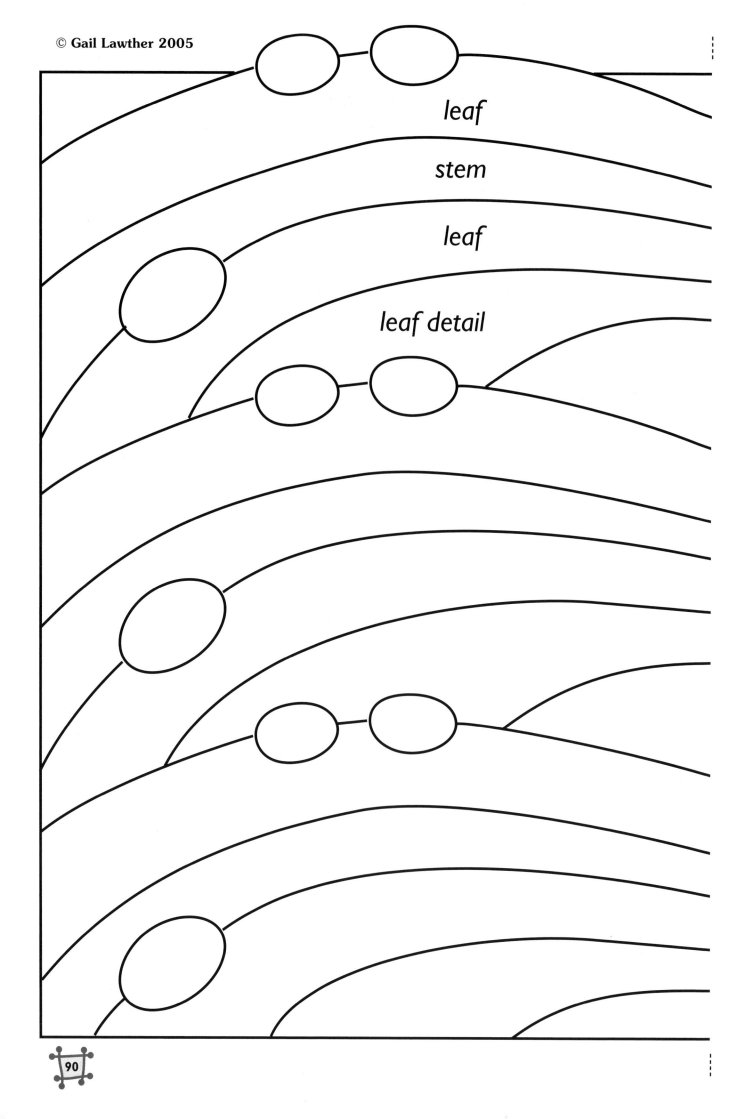

© Gail Lawther 2005

leaf

stem

leaf

leaf detail

90

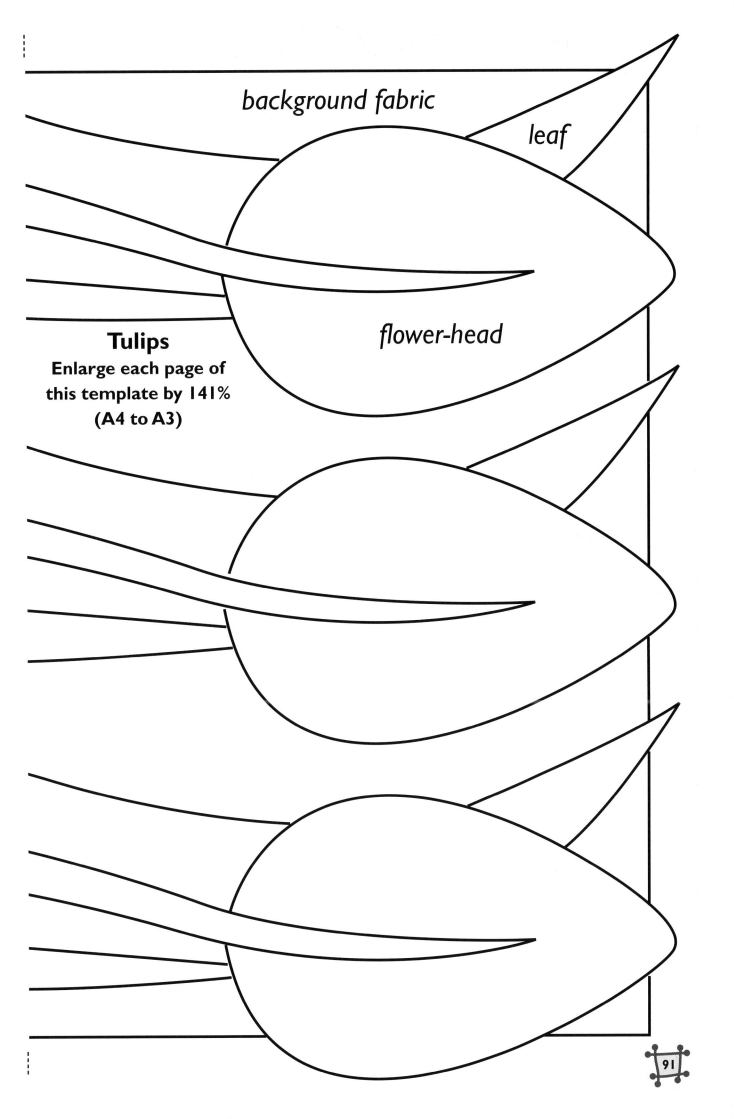

background fabric

leaf

flower-head

Tulips
Enlarge each page of
this template by 141%
(A4 to A3)

Church Window

These templates are full size

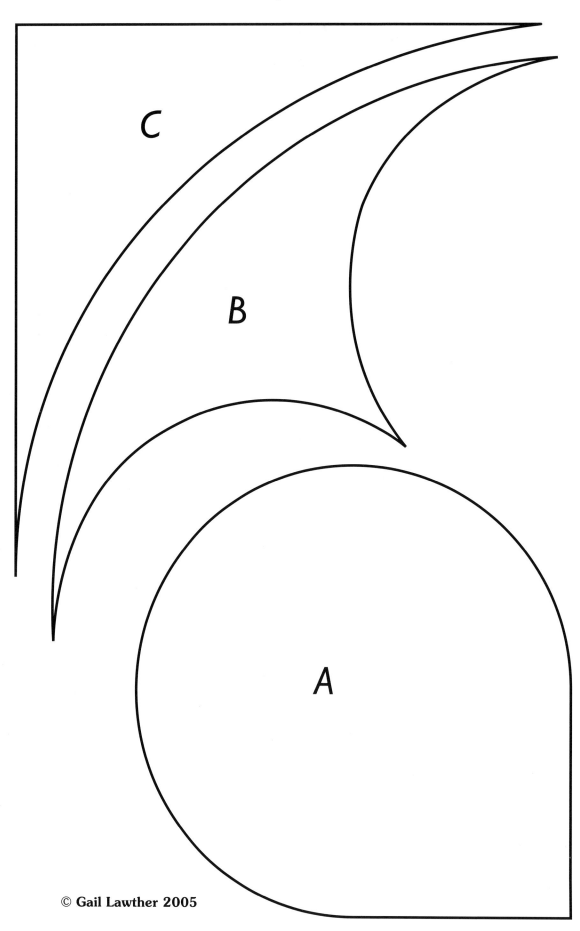

C

B

A

© Gail Lawther 2005

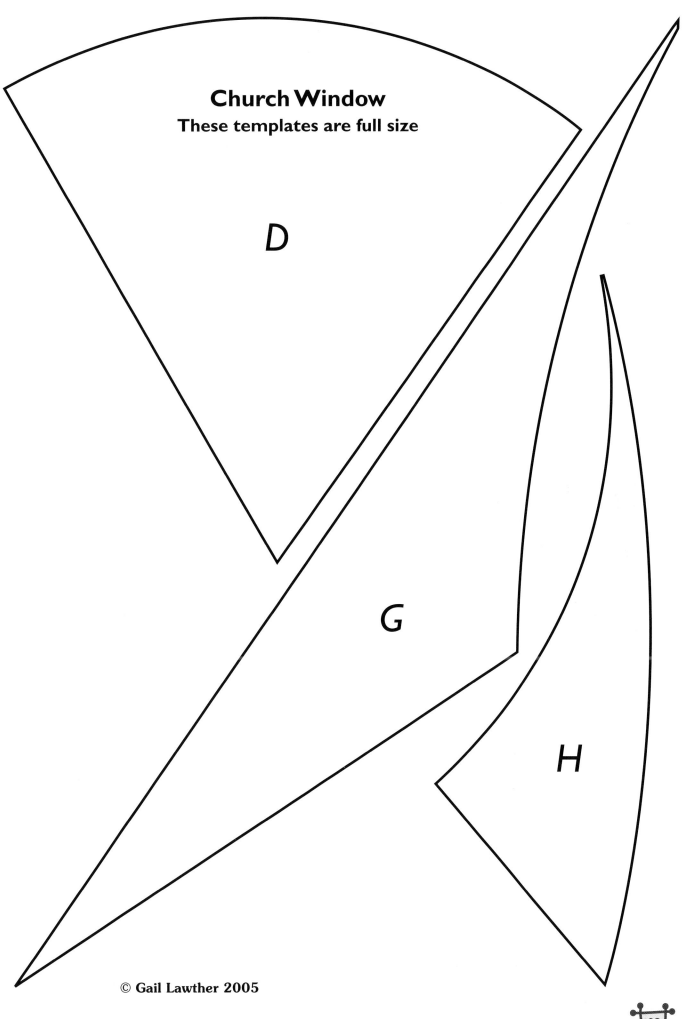

Church Window
These templates are full size

D

G

H

© Gail Lawther 2005

93

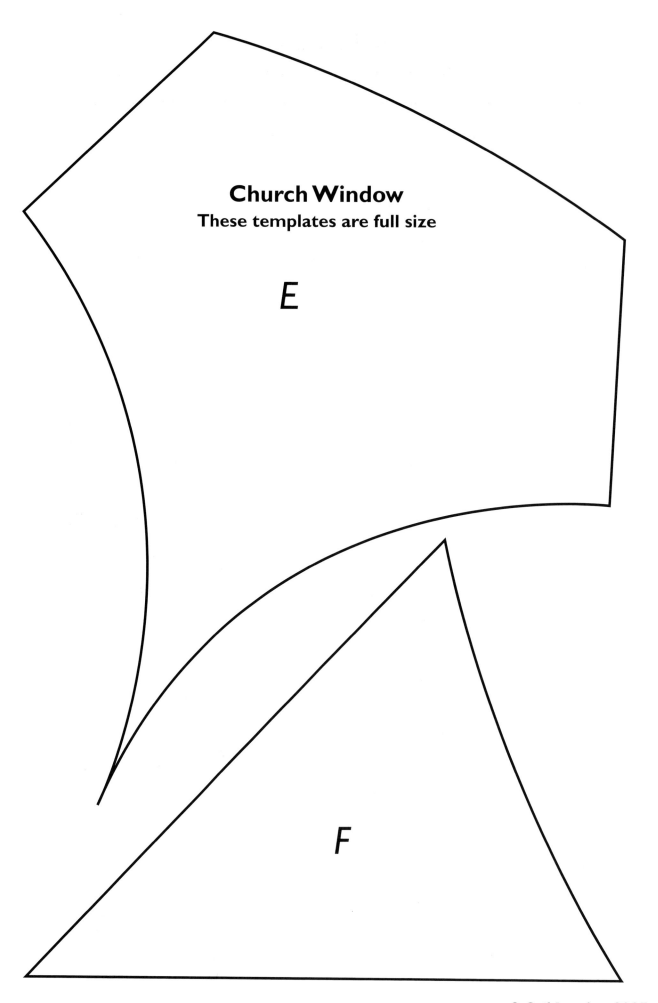

Church Window
These templates are full size

E

F

© Gail Lawther 2005

Iris Landscape

Enlarge the design so that each square measures 4in (10cm)

95

Herb Cushion
These templates are full size

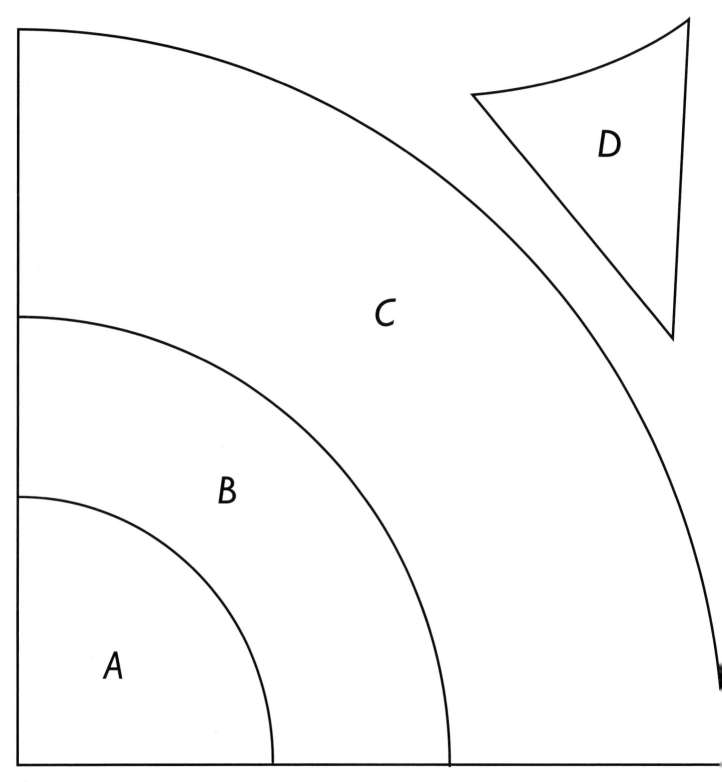

A

B

C

D

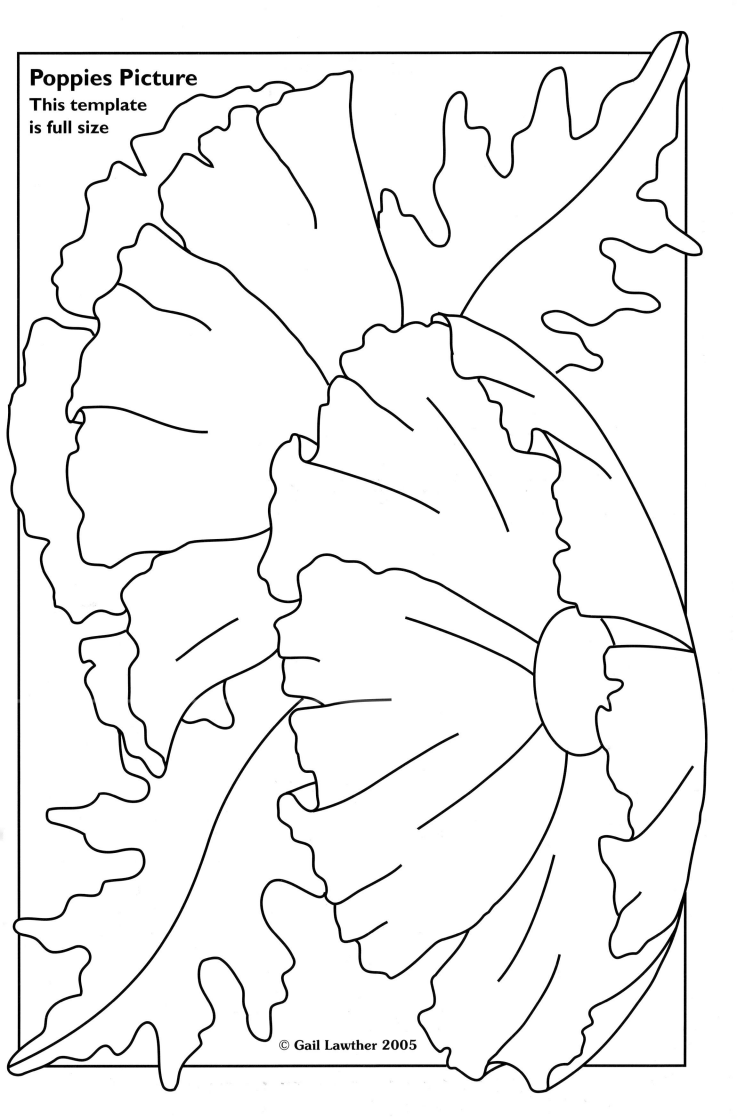

Poppies Picture

This template
is full size

© Gail Lawther 2005

Art Nouveau Rose

**This template
is full size**

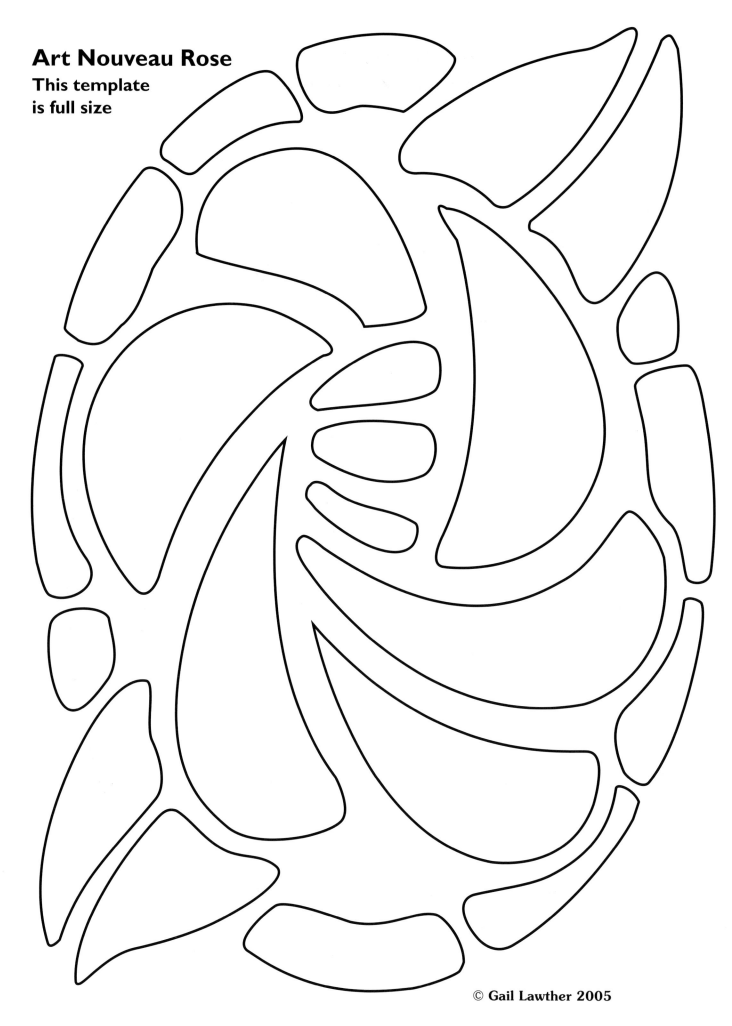

© Gail Lawther 2005

Art Nouveau Rose

These templates are full size

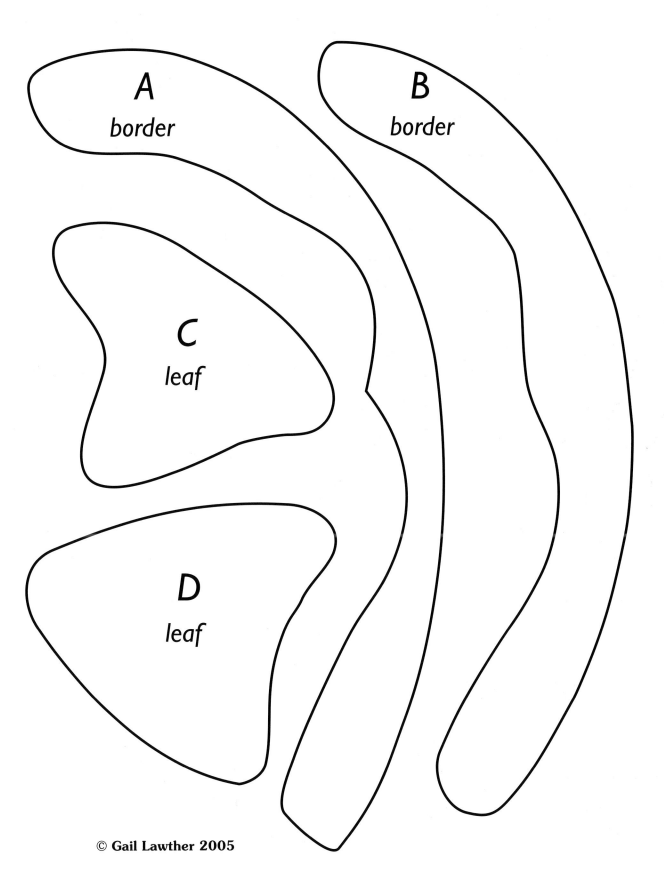

A
border

B
border

C
leaf

D
leaf

© Gail Lawther 2005

It's A Jungle Out There ...
Enlarge the design so that each square measures 5in (13cm)

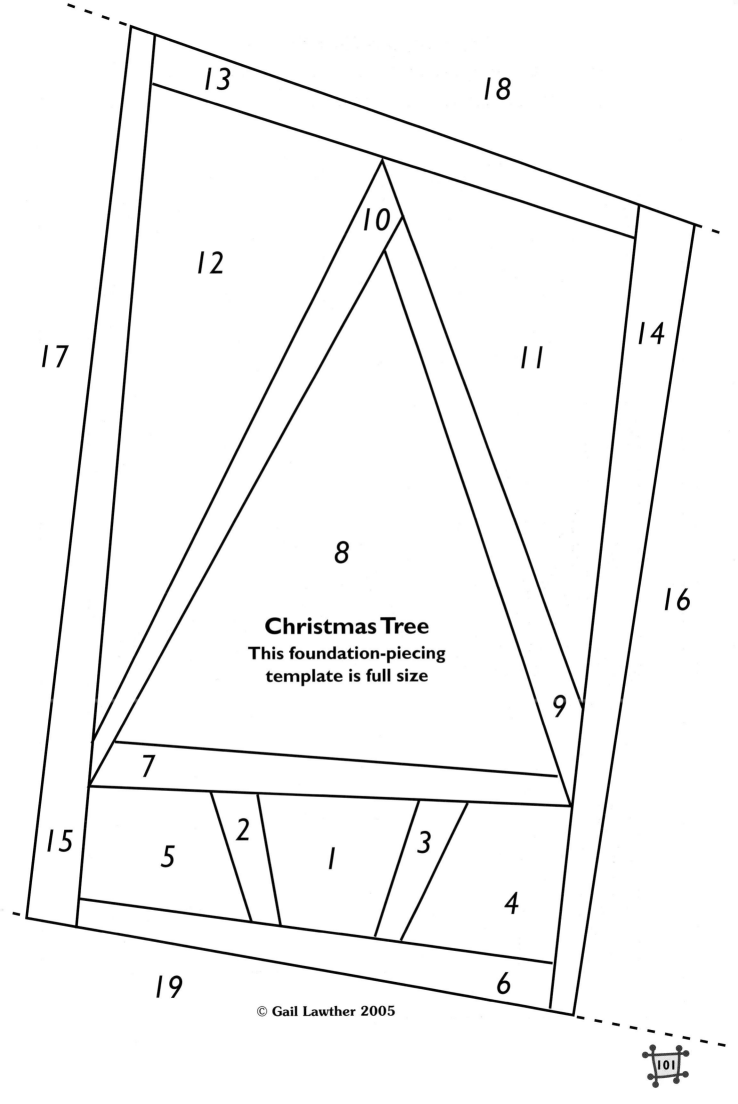

Christmas Tree

This foundation-piecing template is full size

© Gail Lawther 2005

Seascape
This foundation-piecing template is full size

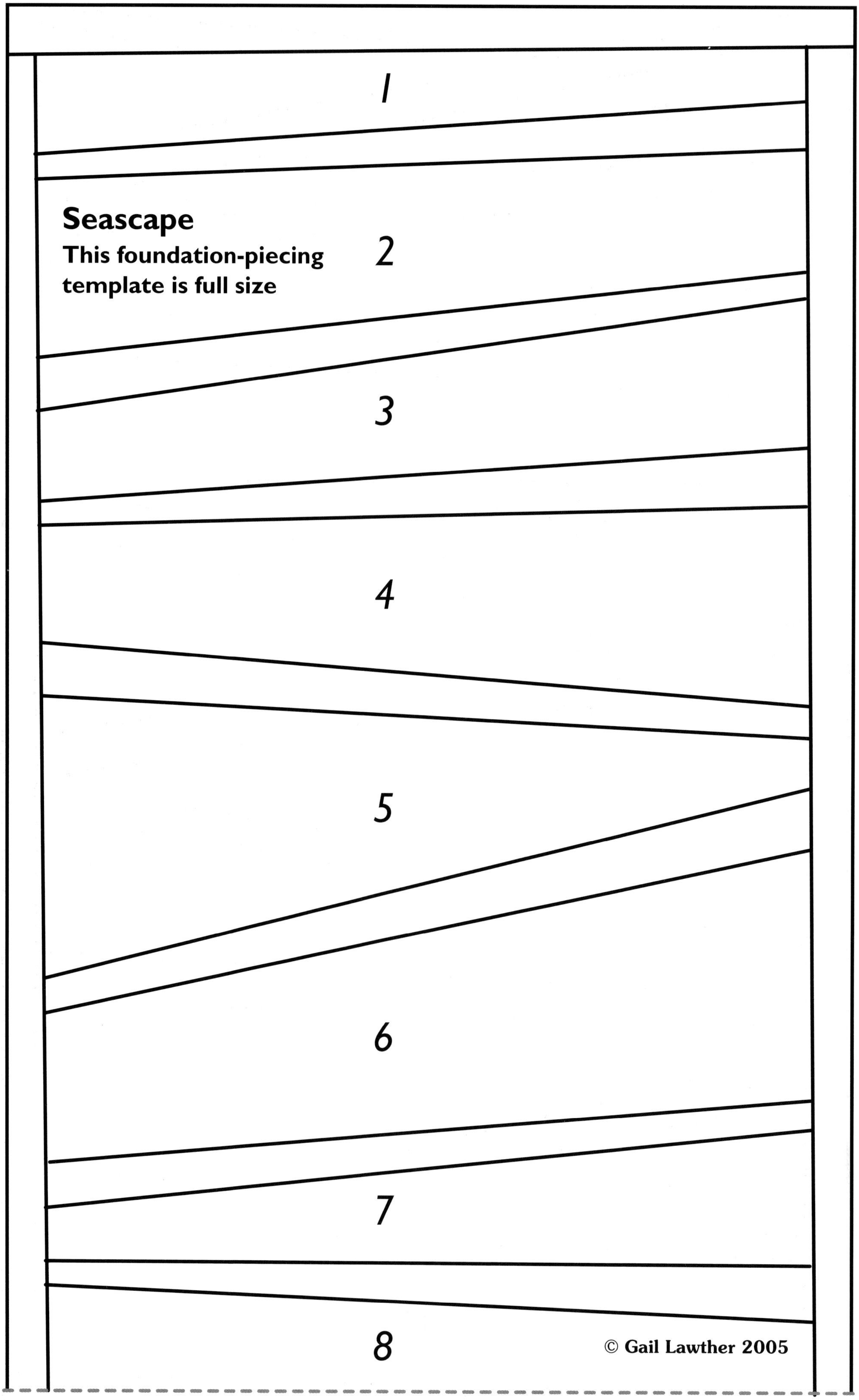

1

2

3

4

5

6

7

8

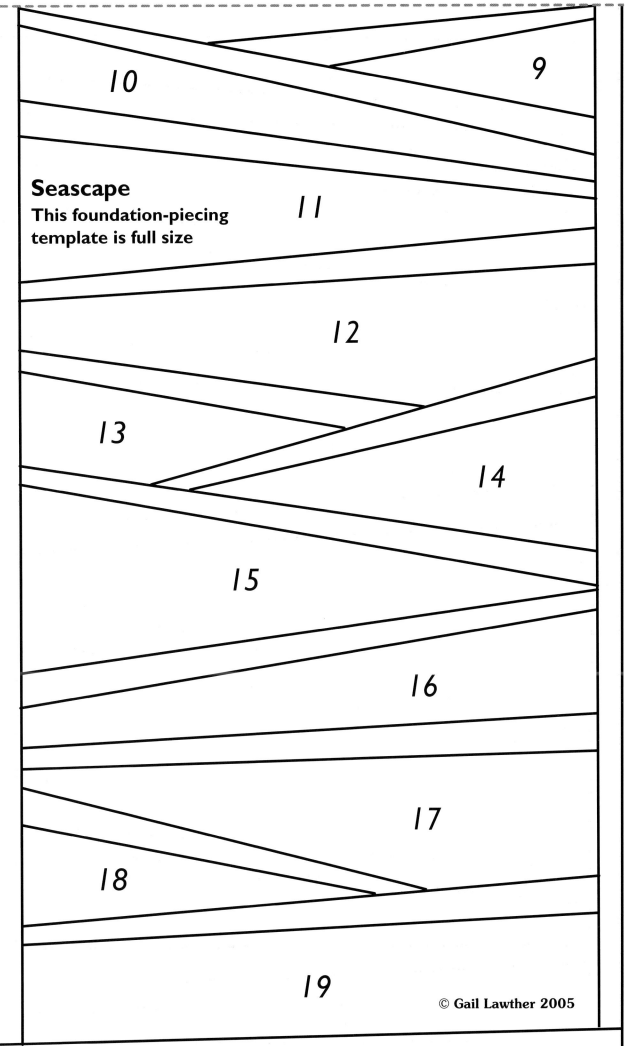

Seascape
This foundation-piecing template is full size

© Gail Lawther 2005

Thankyous and Contact Details

Many thanks to:

Jenny Coleman, whose hands appear in the photographic sequences

Rachel Leadbeater, for her stitching on the bonbon cushions and jungle scene

Diane and Trevor Vellacott, who own the *Iris Landscape*
and let us use their house as a location

Books and patterns

Teamwork Craftbooks also publishes other titles by Gail Lawther:

Showpieces
a colourful gallery of quilts and the stories behind their creation
price £8, including p&p

A Trip Around the World
patchwork and quilting projects inspired by different countries
price £12, including p&p

We also produce many *stained glass patchwork pattern packs.*

Talks and workshops

Gail is also available to do talks, workshops and area days
for quilting groups in the UK and overseas.

TEAMWORK
CRAFTBOOKS

Christopher & Gail Lawther

44 Rectory Walk, Sompting, Lancing, West Sussex, England BN15 0DU

www.gail-quilts-plus.co.uk   thelawthers@ntlworld.com